DEVON AND CORNWALL RECORD SOCIETY

New Series

Volume 68

Frontispiece. Four scenes from the Luttrell Psalter (© BL Add MS 42130) from the British Library archive: fol. 74v (threshing scene), fol. 171r (harrowing with horse), fol. 172v (harvest scene), fol. 173r (stacking sheaves). Early fourteenth century.

THE LANDS
OF A MEDIEVAL
DEVON NUNNERY

The Extents of Canonsleigh Abbey
(Harleian MS no. 3660)
A Translation

Edited with an Introduction by
Des Atkinson

Yorkist
History
Trust

DEVON AND CORNWALL RECORD SOCIETY

BOYDELL PUBLISHING SERVICES

First published 2026

A publication of the
Devon and Cornwall Record Society
supported by Boydell Publishing Services
an imprint of Boydell & Brewer Ltd

PO Box 9, Woodbridge, Suffolk IP12 3DF, UK
and of Boydell & Brewer Inc.
668 Mt Hope Avenue, Rochester, NY 14620–2731, USA
website: www.boydellandbrewer.com

Our Authorised Representative for product safety in the EU
is Easy Access System Europe –
Mustamäe tee 50, 10621 Tallinn, Estonia,
gpsr.requests@easproject.com

ISBN   978 0 90185 365 3

Series information is printed at the back of this volume

A CIP catalogue record for this book is available
from the British Library

The publisher has no responsibility for the continued existence or accuracy
of URLs for external or third-party internet websites referred to in this book,
and does not guarantee that any content on such websites is,
or will remain, accurate or appropriate

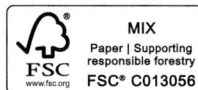

FSC
www.fsc.org
MIX
Paper | Supporting
responsible forestry
FSC® C013056

Printed and bound in Great Britain by
TJ Books, Padstow, Cornwall

CONTENTS

ILLUSTRATIONS

Maps

Tables

Figures

Preface and Acknowledgements

In 1965, the cartulary of Canonsleigh Abbey was calendared and published for the Devon and Cornwall Record Society (DCRS) by Vera London. That publication inspired me to take Canonsleigh as the subject for my MPhil thesis in 2012/13. The cartulary was, however, only part of the manuscript source that Vera London used (Harleian MS no. 3660 in the British Library). The extents or survey of Canonsleigh's lands taken in 1323 were only referred to by her in general terms. Once my master's thesis was over, I had always hoped to come back to those extents and make them as broadly available as the cartulary itself. Now at last this publication fulfils that aspiration. As well as providing the text of the extents in an English translation, I also wanted to produce a full transcription of the Latin text for one of Canonsleigh's manors. Appendix 1 provides this for the manor of Netherton, together with a full English translation. I hope this will prove helpful to others – I know that I have greatly benefitted from similar work by earlier scholars.

I am very grateful to the DCRS for supporting me in this endeavour and in particular to Professor Catherine Rider in her role as the Honorary Editor. She has provided excellent feedback and focus, and this work would never have been completed without her. My very special thanks must go to Dr Oliver Padel, who has given so generously of his time to review my translations of the original text. His expertise on medieval Devon has also been invaluable, and his feedback over many months has greatly improved the final text – thank you Oliver!

The staff at the British Library, the Devon Heritage Centre, the Essex Record Office and the National Archives deserve my grateful thanks. They are all invariably helpful, courteous and highly professional in their work. No scholarly task such as this could be completed without their excellent support.

The DCRS are very grateful for the financial support provided by the Friends of Devon's Archives and the Yorkist History Trust. Their generosity ensures that the DCRS can continue to plan future publications with confidence and know that the finances remain in good shape for the coming years.

I have visited the site of Canonsleigh on numerous occasions, and there are some interesting late medieval remains to be seen, as discussed in the Introduction. A visit I found particularly valuable and stimulating was one hosted by the Tiverton Archaeological Group and led by Dr Stuart Blaylock. Stuart's compendious knowledge and expertise helped to clarify the possible layout of the abbey, even though no proper archaeological survey has ever been undertaken.

Des Atkinson

March 2025

ABBREVIATIONS

BL	The British Library, London
BRUC	A. B. Emden, *A Biographical Register of the University of Cambridge to 1500* (Cambridge: Cambridge University Press, 1963)
BRUO	A. B. Emden, *A Biographical Register of the University of Oxford to A.D.1500*, 3 vols (Oxford: Clarendon Press, 1957–59)
Cartulary	*The Cartulary of Canonsleigh Abbey: Harleian MS.No.3660. A Calendar*, ed. by Vera C. M. London, Devon and Cornwall Record Society Publications, 8 (Torquay: Devon and Cornwall Record Society, 1965)
CPL	*Calendar of Papal Letters*
CPR	*Calendar of Patent Rolls*
DHC	Devon Heritage Centre, Exeter
DLS	Audrey M. Erskine, *The Devonshire Lay Subsidy of 1332*, Devon and Cornwall Record Society Publications. New Series, 14 (Torquay: Devon and Cornwall Record Society, 1969)
ELS	Jennifer C. Ward, *The Medieval Essex Community: The Lay Subsidy of 1327*, Essex Historical Documents, 1 (Essex: Essex Record Office, 1983)
ERO	Essex Record Office, Chelmsford
£ s d	Pounds (*libre*), shillings (*solidi*) and pence (*denarii*); 12 pence to a shilling, 20 shillings to a pound
Latham	R. E. Latham, *Revised Medieval Latin Word-List from British and Irish Sources* (Oxford: Oxford University Press, 1965)
LP	*Letters and Papers Foreign & Domestic of the Reign of Henry VIII*, ed. J. S. Brewer et al., 22 vols in 35 (London: Longman, Green, Longman and Roberts, 1862–1932)
MUL	Manchester University Library
n.d.	No date
ODNB	*Oxford Dictionary of National Biography*
Reg. Bronescombe	*The Registers of Walter Bronescombe (A.D. 1257–1280), and Peter Quivil (A.D. 1280–1291), Bishops of Exeter, with Some Records of the Episcopate of Bishop Thomas de Bytton (A.D. 1291–1307); Also the Taxation of Pope Nicholas IV. A.D. 1291 – (Diocese of Exeter)*, ed. by F. C. Hingeston (Covent Garden: George Bell & Sons, York Street, 1889)

Reg. Grandisson	*The Register of John de Grandisson, Bishop of Exeter, (A.D. 1327–1369)*, ed. by F. C. Hingeston-Randolph, 3 vols (Covent Garden: George Bell & Sons, York Street, 1894–9)
Reg. Stafford	*The Register of Edmund Stafford (A.D. 1395–1419): An Index and Abstract of Its Contents.*, ed. by F. C. Hingeston (London: Eland, 1886)
Reg. Stapledon	*The Register of Walter de Stapeldon, Bishop of Exeter (A.D. 1307–1326)*, ed. by F. C. Hingeston-Randolph (London: G. Bell, 1892)
Taxatio	*Taxatio Ecclesiastica Angliae et Walliae Auctoritate P. Nicholai IV. circa A.D. 1291*, ed. by T. Astle, S. Ayscough, and J. Caley (London: George Eyre and Andrew Strahan, Printers, 1802). See also *Taxatio* online at https://www.dhi.ac.uk/taxatio/
TNA	The National Archives, Kew
Valor	*Valor Ecclesiasticus*, ed. by J. Caley and the Rev. J. Hunter, 6 vols, 1810–34

INTRODUCTION

The fourteenth century was a time of great change and stress in the English countryside. The whole of Devon was radically affected by the mid-century catastrophe of the Black Death.[1] However, even by the first quarter of the century, the impact of failed harvests and widespread animal disease was putting great pressure on the rural landscape. The relatively benign climate of the thirteenth century was giving way to much more unsettled conditions. The population of England had been growing significantly, and now this changing environment was causing strain and difficulty in the south-west of England and beyond. Rural life at this time was centred on the manor, the unit of administration that governed the annual rhythm of communities such as those under the control of Canonsleigh Abbey, one of the three medieval nunneries in Devon.[2] Like all monastic communities, Canonsleigh relied strongly on its endowment of manors to provide it with a stable financial base to fulfil its eternal function of prayer for the salvation of souls. In the context of the early fourteenth century, with its new stresses and difficulties, Canonsleigh was not well prepared. It did not appear to have a clear understanding of its manorial possessions, and, by 1319, the abbess appears to have been old and ailing.

In 1320, a new abbess had been elected, and the bishop of Exeter, Walter de Stapledon, was taking a close and supportive interest in the nunnery. He seems to have decided that a proper survey of the abbey's possessions was needed, and so the extents of Canonsleigh were produced in the summer of 1323. That survey or set of extents was compiled alongside a listing of all the land charters and other documents that defined the possessions of Canonsleigh, a document known as a cartulary.[3] These manorial extents are a rich source of information about the nature of rural life in Devon at this time. They show us the size and type of Canonsleigh's 'demesne', the lands managed directly by the abbey to support its religious life.[4] We can see what types of crops were being grown and the value of those outputs. They also provide a listing of the tenants who held land within Canonsleigh's manors, whether as free or bonded tenants. The holding of a bonded tenancy required their holders to undertake a series of services for their manorial lady, the abbess. These services are listed in detail within the extents and were often onerous. As well as the names of the tenants, the extents show us the size of their tenant holdings and the amount of rent and other payments they were required to render to their landlord.

---

[1] The Black Death arrived in England in June 1348; within a year, it had infected the whole of the country.

[2] Canonsleigh, a house for Augustinian canonesses, was the largest of the three and was located in east Devon near the village of Burlescombe. The others were Cornworthy Priory near Totnes, another Augustinian house, and Polsloe Priory near Exeter, a nunnery of the Benedictine order.

[3] In 1965, Vera London produced an edition of the cartulary for the DCRS. In her introduction, London provides a very useful history of the abbey. See: *The Cartulary of Canonsleigh Abbey: Harleian MS.No.3660. A Calendar*, ed. by Vera C. M. London, DCRS Publications, 8 (DCRS, 1965).

[4] See the Glossary for the definition of terms such as 'demesne'.

They provide us with a good understanding of the overall value of Canonsleigh's manorial endowment, something we only see again with the *Valor Ecclesiasticus* of Henry VIII some two hundred years later.[5]

Canonsleigh's extents therefore tell us much about rural life in Devon, but they also extended to other parts of England. One fascinating aspect of Canonsleigh's history had been the patronage of the very wealthy Matilda de Clare, the countess of Gloucester and Hertford, who had re-founded Canonsleigh as a nunnery in the 1280s. She had granted additional lands to the abbey, including some of her possessions in Essex and Suffolk. These eastern properties are also listed within the extents and include not just rural possessions but also the Essex borough of Manningtree. The differing social make-up of those eastern possessions with their higher proportion of free tenants provides a contrast to manors such as Dunsford in Devon with their much higher proportion of bonded tenants.

The extents of Canonsleigh Abbey therefore provide us with a rich snapshot of people, life, society and economy across a broad geographical area. It is not common to have such a clear and detailed picture of late medieval communities, especially in these decades shortly before the Black Death. This publication contains an English version of the extents, providing a clear and approachable rendering of the original fourteenth-century manuscript. It should be of value to a wide range of readers with an interest in the history and people of Devon and beyond.

The Location, Possessions and History of Canonsleigh Abbey

The rural site of Canonsleigh Abbey lies around 17 miles north-east of Exeter near the county border between Devon and Somerset.[6] East Devon today is today an area of rich pastureland with more rugged grazing on its rolling hillsides and on the higher ground of the Blackdown and Brendon hills. In medieval times, the area contained a significant proportion of arable land, though during the later medieval period there was a steady transition from arable to pastoral agriculture, which can be traced particularly clearly at Tavistock Abbey.[7] Canonsleigh is situated beside a small river on a level site at 400 feet above sea level, with higher ground sheltering it to the north. Less than a mile to the south of the Canonsleigh site is the small village of Burlescombe with its church. The closest medieval urban settlements were the small towns of Tiverton to the west and Wellington to the east across the Somerset border, both around 5 miles away.[8] The site today is much altered from the medieval period. The area is now called Canonsleigh Farm and is a jumble of agricultural and domestic buildings. There are few physical remains of the abbey. The small fifteenth-century gatehouse, which is the only building to survive relatively intact,

---

[5] The *Valor* was a major administrative exercise commissioned by Henry VIII in 1535. It contains very detailed information on the possessions and income of all the religious houses in England. Similar information was gathered for the rest of the English Church. For the level of detail it contains and the speed of its production, it was a 'staggering achievement' (Diarmaid MacCulloch, *Thomas Cromwell: A Life* (Allen Lane, 2018), p. 275).

[6] Vera London provides a very good introduction to the geography and chronology of Canonsleigh, and much of this section is based on her work (*Cartulary*, pp. ix–xiv).

[7] W. G. Hoskins, *Devon* (Phillimore, 2003), p. 95; H. P. R. Finberg, *Tavistock Abbey: A Study in the Social and Economic History of Devon* (Kelley, 1969), p. 158.

[8] For details of their borough status see Maurice Beresford, *English Medieval Boroughs: A Hand-List* (David and Charles, 1973), pp. 99, 159.

Map 1. The Location of Canonsleigh Abbey.

is situated at the western end of the site. A long way to the east is a stretch of long wall, and by the small river are the massive remains of a building that are almost certainly part of the reredorter.[9] These buildings are built using the local limestone, as is the church at Burlescombe where Beer and Ham Hill stone have been used to dress the structure.[10] No detailed archaeological survey of the abbey site has yet been undertaken or published, so the layout of the conventual buildings is unclear. The historical record describes a conventual church, a cloister, the chapter house, the room of the abbess, an upper chamber, a house for the abbess (at least by the year 1447), an infirmary and its chapel, another 'large chapel' and some mills.[11]

[9] Elworthy, writing in 1892, states that the ruin provided clear evidence of it being a reredorter – F.T. Elworthy, 'Canonsleigh', *Reports and Transactions of the Devonshire Association* 24 (1892): pp. 359–76 (pp. 360–1).
[10] Bridget Cherry, *The Buildings of England: Devon/by Bridget Cherry and Nikolaus Pevsner* (Yale University Press, 2004), p. 239.
[11] Details gleaned from the cartulary and from the registers of the bishops of Exeter. In 1793, the large chapel is described as having been knocked down a few years before (Richard Polwhele, *The History of Devonshire* (Printed by Trewman and Son, for Cadell, Johnson, and Dilly, London, 1793), p. 369 – it is possible that the abbey church was being described). See also Cherry, *The Buildings of England:Devon*, p. 243.

Fig. 1. The abbey gatehouse at Canonsleigh (the aspect from outside the abbey precinct). Photo taken by the author.

Fig. 2. The reredorter (latrine block) at Canonsleigh. Photo by the author.

Foundation and Re-foundation

The chronology of Canonsleigh is eventful. The brief overview provided here is designed to place the subsequent sections into context. Canonsleigh was founded as a priory for Augustinian canons in about the year 1160 under the patronage of Walter de Clavile, lord of Burlescombe.[12] It fell under the jurisdiction of the bishops of Exeter, since the parish of Burlescombe in which Canonsleigh lies is in the diocese of Exeter and the deanery of Tiverton. The canons appear to have had a problematic history, and in 1284 they were evicted from the priory when it was re-founded under the patronage of Matilda de Clare, the widowed – and exceptionally wealthy – countess of Gloucester and Hertford. The new abbey was dedicated to the Blessed Virgin Mary, St John the Evangelist and St Etheldreda and was to be a house of prayer for the soul of the late husband of the countess.[13] There was acrimony at the time of the new foundation, and for the next fifteen years the canons struggled unsuccessfully to regain their possessions.[14]

In 1284, the newly arrived nuns would have benefitted from the existing buildings and associated facilities, but the income they needed had not yet been provided. In August 1285, the bishop of Exeter acknowledged the receipt of 600 marks from the countess as a security until she could complete the purchase and transfer of lands and rents.[15] However, that money was not released to the nuns for many years – it had been seized by King Edward I, who was always seeking resources to finance his military campaigns – and the full endowment took almost thirty years to be completed.

The new house was intended for forty Augustinian canonesses, and it inherited all of the endowment of the priory. However, by August 1314 it appears the number may have been as high as fifty.[16] Bishop Stapledon praised the nuns greatly and stated that 'their fame and renown had gone out to all the borders of the kingdom of England'.[17] It seems that Canonsleigh was therefore drawing in religious women from a wide area. In April 1356, shortly after the first terrible outbreak of the Black Death, the abbey was once again a popular centre, although this time the bishop (John Grandisson) was less happy. He complained of secular individuals coming into the abbey precinct, stating that people from nearby parishes had been coming

---

[12] *Cartulary*, 12 (pp. 2–3). His overlord was the earl of Gloucester.

[13] Eileen Power uses the alternative name of St. Audrey (Eileen Power, *Medieval English Nunneries: c. 1275 to 1535* (Cambridge University Press, 1922), p. 686). Dockray-Miller lists the various usages as Aethelthryth, Etheldreda or Audrey (see Mary Dockray-Miller, *Saints Edith and Æthelthryth: Princesses, Miracle Workers, and Their Late Medieval Audience; The Wilton Chronicle and The Wilton Life of St Æthelthryth*, Medieval Women: Texts and Contexts; vol. 25 (Brepols, 2009), p. 3).

[14] *Cartulary*, pp. xii–xiii. The monks engaged the support of Archbishop Pecham of Canterbury, and there was something of a stand-off between him and Bishop Quivil of Exeter. Only after intervention by Pope Nicholas IV in 1299 was the case finally settled in favour of the nunnery.

[15] A mark was two-thirds of a pound, i.e. 13 shillings and 4 pence.

[16] *Reg. Stapledon*, p. 94 where the bishop talks of *sustentacionem Canonicarum in numero quiquagenario* (the support of canonesses fifty in number). We have no further information as to the number of nuns until 1410 when there were ten nuns present to elect a new abbess (*Reg. Stafford*, pp. 48–9). By the time the abbey was suppressed in 1539, the number of nuns had recovered somewhat to eighteen (Lawrence S. Snell, *The Suppression of the Religious Foundations of Devon and Cornwall* (Wordens of Cornwall Limited, 1967), p. 126).

[17] *Reg. Stapledon*, p. 94.

into the nunnery, especially on Sundays and feast days to attend divine service. It may be that the nuns' sanctity drew them in, perhaps aided by their singing during the mass.[18]

At the time of the foundation, the countess said she was prepared to endow the nuns with an income of £200 per year.[19] Additional lands and spiritualities were granted by the countess and her descendants. The first three canonesses came from the sister Augustinian house at Lacock, and the numbers at the abbey appear to have grown rapidly. An important early event was the death without issue in 1314 of the abbey's patron, Gilbert de Clare, at the battle of Bannockburn. The patronage then passed by marriage to the Despenser family for a century, before eventually ending up in the hands of the crown in 1487.[20]

The early fourteenth century was probably the zenith of Canonsleigh Abbey's existence. Very quickly, the abbey's fortunes appear to have deteriorated. The abbey's cartulary was written in 1323 during the episcopate of Walter de Stapledon in response to financial problems. Stapledon may well have been the driving force behind its production, and it is noteworthy that most of its entries begin with a summary in French that could easily be read by the abbess. By 1323, the abbey's possessions were almost complete, so the cartulary is a very important document in relating Canonsleigh's financial history.

The broader historical record for Canonsleigh is at times frustratingly quiet. There is no detailed evidence of the impact on the house of that great famine of the early fourteenth century,[21] or of the Black Death. There is more information from the fifteenth century, where we can see the number of nuns falling as low as ten but rising towards the Dissolution in 1539, at which time there were eighteen nuns including the abbess. The list of names of the abbesses is almost complete, and it is notable that two of them occupied their position for forty years.[22] Although in 1535 the income of the abbey as shown in the *Valor Ecclesiasticus* was a little under the £200 threshold required by the statute of 1536 for the house to continue, it was granted leave to do so on payment of a £200 fine.[23] The surrender of the abbey to the commissioners of the king took place on 16 February 1539.[24] In March 1547, the abbey site came into the possession of Sir John St Leger.[25]

---

[18] *Reg. Grandisson*, ii, pp. 1185–6.

[19] *CPL*, i, p. 478.

[20] Henry VII seized the abbey from the widow of Richard Neville – *Cartulary*, p. xiv.

[21] 'The Great Famine lasted from 1315 to 1322. After a disastrous harvest in 1315 this was a period of poor yields and animal murrain. It has been described as an agrarian crisis' (see I. Kershaw, 'The Great Famine and Agrarian Crisis in England 1315–1322', in *Peasants, Knights and Heretics: Studies in Medieval English Social History*, ed. by R. H. Hilton (Cambridge University Press, 1976), pp. 85–132).

[22] Smith, *The Heads of Religious Houses*, vol. 2, pp. 549–50, vol. 3, pp. 634–5.

[23] *LP*, XIII.ii, p. 177 (no. 457).

[24] William Dugdale, *Monasticon Anglicanum: A History of the Abbies and Other Monasteries ... and Cathedral and Collegiate Churches ... in England and Wales*, new edn by John Caley, Henry Ellis and Bulkeley Bandinel, 8 vols (Longman, Hurst, 1817), vol. VI, p. 334.

[25] *CPR*, Edward VI, i, pp. 263–5.

The Possessions

The temporal possessions of Canonsleigh – its landed possessions – were mostly in Devon and neighbouring Somerset.[26] However, there was also an important manor at Sheddon in Essex that contained the small town of Manningtree; it was given by Matilda de Clare, as was some land in Suffolk and several possessions in the city of Exeter.

Table 1. Canonsleigh Abbey's temporal possessions.[27]

Name of manor	Parish	Date entered Canonsleigh's possession	References
Leigh	Burlescombe, Devon	By 1177	*Cartulary*, 12
Dunsford	Dunsford, Devon	From *c.* 1291	*Cartulary*, 271
Gusford	Belstead, Suffolk	By 1312	*Cartulary*, 219
Hockford Waters	Hockworthy, Devon	From *c.* 1293	*Cartulary*, 261
Manningtree	Mistley, Essex	By 1311	*Cartulary*, 221
Netherton	Farway, Devon	By 1177	*Cartulary*, 12
Northleigh	Northleigh, Devon	From *c.* 1313	*Cartulary*, 266–7
Rockbeare	Rockbeare, Devon	By 1289	*Cartulary*, 262
Sampford Arundel	Sampford Arundel, Somerset	By 1224	*Cartulary*, 121
Sheddon	Mistley, Essex	From 1286	*Cartulary*, 207–8
Thorne St Margaret	Thorne St Margaret, Somerset	By *c.* 1243	*Cartulary*, 77–110

The tenant lands amounted to 4,430 acres, and the demesne land to 1,790 acres. There were mills, dovecotes, fishponds, rights of way and the rights to an annual five-day fair at Leigh and a weekly market there. Of their three hundred tenants, around two-thirds were free.

Canonsleigh's spiritual possessions – the churches that were appropriated to Canonsleigh with their associated incomes – made up around one-quarter of the nunnery's value at the time of the *Valor Ecclesiasticus*.[28]

---

[26] Much of the information for this paragraph is taken from *Cartulary*, p. xv.

[27] This and the following table are based closely on the data contained in M. Jurkowski and others, *English Monastic Estates, 1066–1540: A List of Manors, Churches and Chapels*, Special Series; vols 40–2, 3 vols (List and Index Society, 2007), vol. i, pp. 62–3.

[28] By appropriation is meant the transfer of the endowment, or part of the endowment, of a parish church to a religious institution. It would provide income from tithes, offerings and other fees as well as possession of the glebe land.

Table 2. Canonsleigh Abbey's spiritual possessions.

Type	Property	Parish	Tenure	References
Church	Burlescombe	Burlescombe, Devon	By 1177; approp. by 1282	*Cartulary*, 12, 32
Church	Dowland	Dowland, Devon	by 1177; approp. by 1238	*Cartulary*, 12, 32, 142
Church	Dunsford	Dunsford, Devon	From *c.* 1291; approp. by 1314	*Cartulary*, 271, 276
Church	East Morden	Morden, Dorset	By 1177; approp. by 1262	*Cartulary*, 12, 133
Church	Hockworthy	Hockworthy, Devon	By 1201; approp. 1202	*Cartulary*, 144, 154; *Reg. Bronescombe*, ii, p. 73 (item 1029, December 1274)
Church	Little Hempstone	Hempstone, Devon	By 1264	*Cartulary*, 127–8, 131
Church	Northleigh	Northleigh, Devon	moiety, prob. from *c.* 1313	*Cartulary*, p. xv, nos. 266–70
Church	Rockbeare	Rockbeare, Devon	By 1289; approp. 1333	*Cartulary*, 262
Church	Sampford Arundel	Sampford Arundel, Somerset	By 1204; approp. by 1205	*Cartulary*, 110, 114–15
Chapel	All Saints, Canonsleigh	Burlescombe, Devon	By 1539	*Cartulary*, p. xv
Chapel	Holy Trinity, West Leigh	Burlescombe, Devon	By 1539	*Cartulary*, p. xv
Chapel	St Cyr	Cruwys Morchard, Devon	By 1439	*Reg. Lacy* (ed. Dunstan), ii, p. 149
Chapel	St Theobald	Burlescombe, Devon	From *c.* 1374	*Reg. Brantyngham*, i, p. 335
Chapel	St Thomas the Martyr, Canonsleigh	Burlescombe, Devon	From *c.* 1389	*Reg Brantyngham*, ii, p. 678

These *spiritualia* were mostly in Devon and Somerset, but there was also the church of East Morden in Dorset, which provided a significant proportion of the spiritual income. Like the temporal possessions, the spiritual possessions were rural ones. The only urban centre of any importance was the small Essex town of Manitre (modern-day Manningtree) in the manor of Sheddon (Mistley parish). In addition to the properties named in Table 2, there was also a little income from the church of Huntsham where '*Abbatissa de Leghe percipit de eadem xij d*' ('the abbess of Leghe gains/secures 12 pence from the same'), according to the *Taxatio* record from 1291.[29]

These possessions made Canonsleigh a relatively wealthy house. In England, there was a total of twenty-two nunneries of the Augustinian order.[30] Canonsleigh was in the top five of those by value in 1535. The richest Augustinian female houses were in London, where Holywell Priory had a net value of £300 and Clerkenwell Priory £262. That was still well below the wealthiest West Country nunnery, the Benedictine house at Shaftesbury in Dorset, which was valued at £1,329.[31] Nonetheless, Canonsleigh was wealthier than many of its counterparts in Devon. As a point of comparison, the following table shows the comparative values of those nunneries closest to Canonsleigh as well as Lacock Abbey (the house from which Canonsleigh had been re-founded as a nunnery). It shows the net values of each house as taken from the *Valor Ecclesiasticus* of 1535.

Table 3. The net value and the number of nuns at Canonsleigh compared to three other nunneries.

Nunnery	Net value in the *Valor*[32]	Number of nuns in the 1530s[33]	Notes
Canonsleigh	£197	18	
Cornworthy	£63	7	Near Totnes, Devon. An Augustinian nunnery.
Lacock	£210	17	Wiltshire. Also an Augustinian nunnery. The net value is from a second valuation made in 1536.
Polsloe	£164	14	Near Exeter, Devon. A Benedictine house.

[29] *Reg. Bronescombe*, App. 2. The *Taxatio* was an ecclesiastical taxation assessment of 1291–2. This was often called the Pope Nicholas IV *Taxatio* because it was carried out on the orders of that pope.

[30] David Knowles and R. Neville Hadcock, *Medieval Religious Houses, England and Wales* (Longmans, Green, 1953), pp. 227–9.

[31] William Page, *The Victoria History of the County of Dorset: Volume 2*, Victoria History of the Counties of England (Constable, 1908), pp. 73–9.

[32] See vol. 2 of the *Valor:* Canonsleigh pp. 328–30; Cornworthy p. 366; Lacock pp. 115–18; Polsloe p. 315.

[33] For Cornworthy, see Lawrence S. Snell, *The Suppression of the Religious Foundations of Devon and Cornwall* (Wordens of Cornwall Limited, 1967), p. 127.

Fig. 3. *The Virgin and Child with an Augustinian Canoness* by a follower of Joos van Cleve. Image NG945 courtesy of the National Gallery, London.

The Extents

The purpose of an extent (*extenta*) was to provide a comprehensive survey and valuation of the demesne lands of a manor, together with the obligations and labour services of the tenantry.[34] The values that were attached were those of yearly income, not the sale value of the particular item.[35] The Canonsleigh extents certainly pass Reginald Lennard's 'real' test that they should give the money value of the demesne lands and services.[36] The extents for the eastern possessions in Essex and Suffolk differ in their headings from those in Devon and Somerset. The eastern possessions begin with the words Extent, Rental and Custumal (*Extenta, Rentale et Custumarium*), whereas the western possessions simply say *Extenta*. The one minor exception is the manor of Hockford Waters – here, the opening words are *Extenta et Custumarius*. In terms of format and contents, the information for Hockford seems little different from that for the other western manors.

Harleian Manuscript 3660 is one of the British Library's select manuscripts and dates principally from 1323.[37] The bound volume contains the cartulary and extents

---

[34] R. E. Latham, *Revised Medieval Latin Word-List from British and Irish Sources* (Published for the British Academy by Oxford University Press, 1965), p. 181.

[35] P. D. A. Harvey, *Manorial Records of Cuxham, Oxfordshire, c. 1200–1359*, Oxfordshire Record Series, 50 (Oxfordshire Record Society, 1976), p. 75.

[36] R. Lennard, 'What Is a Manorial Extent?', *The English Historical Review* 44, no. 174 (1929), pp. 256–63 (p. 261).

[37] The British Library requires readers to have a letter of introduction to view a select manuscript. For further details see https://bl.libguides.com/reference-services/manuscripts/restricted-items [accessed 24 Feb. 2025].

of Canonsleigh. The Cartulary has been edited by Vera London, but the extents
have never been transcribed or translated, receiving only relatively brief mentions
by London.[38] The current publication provides an edition in an English translation
of those extents, summarising their contents. In addition, a fully transcribed copy of
the original Latin text with an English translation is provided for the Devon manor
of Netherton to give an example of the language and format of the extents in their
original form (Appendix 1).

The extents are of particular interest as they provide a picture of life in a medieval
monastic estate in a period some twenty years before the arrival of the Black Death,
when the nunnery was beset by serious challenges. The years 1315–22 were a time
of agrarian crisis.[39] Across southern and eastern England, aggregate demesne sheep
numbers fell by some 30 per cent. A major cattle plague was also felt across England.
Problems were compounded by successive poor harvests and a lack of good animal
fodder. The global climate was clearly deteriorating from the relatively benign
conditions of the mid-thirteenth century. The result was increasing variability in
the weather across north-western Europe, including England, in the first half of the
fourteenth century. Canonsleigh cannot have been immune to these deteriorating
conditions. Furthermore, the financial management of the house under the rule of
the ageing abbess Petronilla de Clare was of such concern that Bishop Stapledon
of Exeter appointed Canoness Joan de Radyngtone as co-adjutor (i.e. someone
appointed to assist an infirm ecclesiastic) in January 1320.[40] The bishop made further
visitations to Canonsleigh, including one in March 1323, when he very possibly
ordered the cartulary and extents to be written.[41]

A thorough description of the manuscript has already been provided by London.[42]
The extents make up folios 141r to 178v inclusive, and they are itemised in Table 4
below.

Table 4. The details for the extents within Harleian MS 3660.

Folios	Manor or item name	Date (1323 unless stated otherwise)	Notes
141r–142v	Netherton in Farway, Devon	Mon., 27 June	Second part of Netherton; for the first part see fols 178r–178v below
143r–145r	Rockbeare, Devon	Tue., 28 June	
145v–148r	Dunsford, Devon	Wed., 29 June	

[38] *Cartulary*, pp. xv, xxxiii.
[39] B. M. S. Campbell, *The Great Transition: Climate, Disease and Society in the Late Medieval World* (Cambridge University Press, 2016), pp. 211–15; I. Kershaw, 'The Great Famine and Agrarian Crisis in England 1315–1322', in *Peasants, Knights and Heretics: Studies in Medieval English Social History*, ed. by R. H. Hilton (Cambridge University Press, 1976), pp. 85–132.
[40] *Reg. Stapledon*, p. 96.
[41] *Cartulary*, p. xiv.
[42] *Cartulary*, pp. xxx–xxxv.

(Table 4 continued)

148v–150v	Hockford Waters, Devon	Sun., 19 June	In the parish of Hockworthy
151r–153v	Sheddon, Essex	Tue., 9 Aug.	First part of Sheddon. In the parish of Mistley
154r–158r	Borough of Manningtree, Essex	Tue., 9 Aug.	Manningtree lies within the manor of Sheddon
158v–162r	Gusford, Suffolk	Thu., 4 Aug.	In the parish of Belstead
162v–163v	Sheddon, Essex	Sept., 1323	Second part of Sheddon
164r	Ordinance by Bishop Stapledon re. vicarage of Burlescombe	20 Nov., 1324	Transcribed in the *Cartulary* at Appendix 1, item XII
164v–165r	Ordinance by Bishop Stapledon re. vicarage of Burlescombe	20 Nov., 1324	Transcribed in the *Cartulary* at Appendix 1, item XIII
165v	Case brought by the prior of Canonsleigh in 1262-63	28 Oct., 1262–12 Feb., 1263	Summarised in the *Cartulary* at Appendix 1, item XIV
166r–166v	Memo re. the appropriated church of Morden, Dorset	1332–c.1335	Summarised in the *Cartulary* at Appendix 1, item XV
167r–175r	Leigh, Devon	Sun., 12 June	Including the extent of Thorne St Margaret, Somerset (at fols 168r–168v)
175v–176r	Sampford Arundel, Somerset	Sun., 12 June	The abbey never held lordship of this manor
176r–177v	Northleigh, Devon	Mon., 27 June	
178r–178v	Netherton in Farway, Devon	Mon., 27 June	First part of Netherton

The extents provide an informative survey of the value of Canonsleigh's possessions some fifty years after it was re-founded as a nunnery. They offer an opportunity to look back at what had been Canonsleigh Priory (if you view just the possessions that the canons had enjoyed at the end of their time there). By making comparison with the *Valor Ecclesiasticus*, compiled over two hundred years later, it also allows us to trace the changes that took place to the house and its endowment over the rest of the Middle Ages. The changing values over time are summarised in the following table. No account has been taken of any change in the value of the pound sterling. The table shows that the proportion of income from spiritualities (i.e. churches appropriated to the abbey) was falling while that from temporalities (the manors and other earthly possessions) was rising.

Table 5. The valuations of Canonsleigh's possessions over its lifetime.

Date	Temporalities (£ and %)	Spiritualities (£ and %)
The priory in 1283	£49 (68%)	£23 (32%)
The abbey in 1323	£113 (76%)	£36 (24%)
The abbey in 1535	£164 (85%)	£29 (15%)

The valuations of 1323 as taken from the extents and those of 1535 in the *Valor Ecclesiasticus* make interesting points of comparison.

Table 6. Comparative values for the Canonsleigh manors.

Manor	Values in 1323	Values in 1535	Notes
Netherton	£9 2s 7½d	£18 14s 11¾d	
Rockbeare	£9 7s 9d	£38 12s 4d	
Dunsford	£17 7s 6½d	£35 15s 6d	
Hockford Waters	£17 9s 3½d	£22 6s 8½d	The 1323 total is an estimate; it includes £3 for the value of the church
Leigh (the home manor)	£34 10s 5¼d	£39 9s 11¾d	Including the value of Chieflowman. The values for the manor of Thorne are incorporated
Sampford Arundel	£6 10s 6d	£2 15s 4d	
Northleigh	-13s 3¾d	Not present	
Sheddon and Manningtree	£28 7s 10½d	£20 0s 5d	
Gusford	£9 4s 5½d	£7 18s 0d	

The changing pattern of these values becomes clearer when viewed graphically (see Fig. 4. below). The values of the Devon manors have increased markedly. By contrast, those for the two manors in eastern England (Sheddon and Manningtree and Gusford) have declined. It is likely that this had happened because instead of trying to manage those distant possessions directly, Canonsleigh opted to lease them out in exchange for a fixed annual income. That Canonsleigh's eastern manors were so distant would have made direct management problematic. In the case of the manor of Sheddon with Manningtree, by 1535 the manor was farmed out to a William Budde by indenture for the term of his life.[43] No transfer of ownership had taken place, and Budde had no hereditary right to pass on that land. Other ecclesiastical landowners in the east of England also leased their estates in the fifteenth century. Rumburgh Priory, Sibton Abbey and Leiston Abbey have all been identified as doing so, and they did so with good reason. A dependency on hired labour in a period when such a resource was scarce and costly provided a significant impetus. Income from a lease was, relatively speaking, of low risk.[44] Meanwhile, Gusford, in Suffolk, was being managed by a seneschal or bailiff.[45] As we have no contemporary accounts or court rolls for Gusford, it is not possible to be sure of the financial arrangements in 1535. Falling rental values for estates in Suffolk in the fifteenth century have been noted, and so here management by a bailiff may have been preferable to leasing.[46]

There were also changes in the nunnery's spiritual possessions between 1323 and 1535. At Sampford Arundel, the income from the church there was a negative value by 1535 as the payment to the perpetual vicar at £6 exceeded the income of £5 6s 10d. At Hockford, the incomplete extent of 1323 did not include income from the church of Hockworthy. That would have been worth probably £3 (720d) before any deductions. That value has therefore been added to the figures given in Table 6. At Rockbeare, the substantial additional income from the church of over £6 is present in 1535. It was not available to the abbey until the appropriation in 1333 – ten years before the extent was compiled – and so does not figure in the 1323 numbers.

The Agricultural Economy

Canonsleigh's lands were therefore largely rural, agricultural ones located nearby in East Devon. In the period 1250 to 1349, Bruce Campbell characterises the cropping system of East Devon as type 5 in his nomenclature. This was a three-course cropping system of wheat and oats. The two cereals were grown in roughly equal proportions within a classic three-course rotation.[47] Geographically, the system was one of the most widely distributed cropping systems in England. We can see from Table 7 that crops such as oats and corn featured in several of the Devon manors. The same cropping system was also common across much of Essex. But further north in Essex and then into Suffolk, Campbell identifies a type 2 system. Here, there was a greater focus on rye with barley, and this pattern is discernible in the table for Canonsleigh's manors of Sheddon and Gusford. Campbell identifies the demesnes that practised the type 2 cropping system as having a strong commercial

---

[43] *Valor*, ii, p. 359.

[44] Mark Bailey, *Medieval Suffolk: An Economic and Social History, 1200–1500* (Boydell & Brewer, 2007), pp. 209–10, doi:10.1017/9781846155710.

[45] 'At farm' means the property was leased out, something that became much more common after the Black Death – Mark Bailey, 'The Transformation of Customary Tenures in Southern England, c. 1350 to c. 1500', *Agricultural History Review* 62, no. 2 (2014), pp. 210–30 (p. 214).

[46] Bailey, *Medieval Suffolk*, p. 232. The reduction on some Suffolk estates was as large as 40 per cent in the period 1420–35 (pp. 207–8).

[47] Campbell, *English Seigniorial Agriculture*, p. 262. Note however that Campbell's sample size of Devon estates is low.

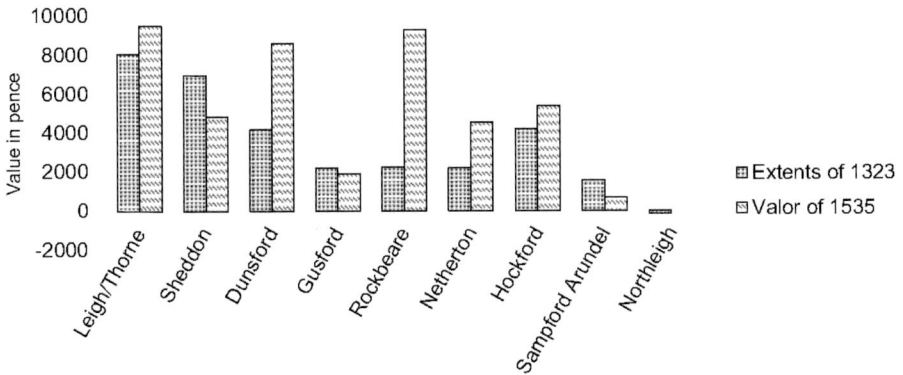

Fig. 4. Canonsleigh's possessions – their changing value over time.

orientation.[48] Among Canonsleigh's western possessions, rye cropping is found only in the small Somerset manor of Sampford Arundel.

Table 7. The list of crops and other resources itemised in each of Canonsleigh's manors.

Manor	Dovecote	Mill(s)	Crops, etc.
Netherton	✓	Water (1)	Alder wood, hay, smithy, wax, oak wood, oats, capon
Rockbeare		Water (1)	
Dunsford	✓		Oak wood
Hockford Waters		Water (1)	Hay, oats, capon
Leigh	✓	Water (3)	Hay, wax, oats, woodcocks, beans, corn, salt, ale, *Chopp'*
Sampford Arundel		Water (1)	Hay, oats, beans, corn, rye, peas
Northleigh			Alder wood, corn, peas
Netherton	✓	Water (1)	Alder wood, hay, corn
Sheddon	✓	Water (1), wind (1)	Alder wood, oars, corn, rye, hens, eggs, peppers, barley
Gusford		Water (1)	Oats, corn, rye, coppice wood, hens, eggs, barley
Manningtree			Smithy, wax, clove

Note: The term *Chopp'* is used only in the extent for Leigh. It appears to be some form of food, but its exact meaning is not clear.

[48] Campbell, *English Seigniorial Agriculture*, p. 268.

Population and Social Composition

In her brief assessment of the numbers of Canonsleigh's tenants, London states that there were about three hundred tenants and that two-thirds were free.[49] This was an underestimate, and a more detailed analysis is provided in Table 8. The total number of tenants is 356, of which 196 were in the western part of Canonsleigh's endowment and 160 in the counties of Essex and Suffolk. In the table, the column headed 'Serfs' includes only those tenants who are specifically described as such, either as *nativus* or *nativa* in the Latin text. They comprise a little over 15 per cent of the total (fifty-four out of the total of 356). That falls well short of the one-third described by London. The explanation lies in those tenants described as free tenants on bonded tenements. These might also be described as customary tenants. Each is characterised as *liber corpore* (free in body) in the Latin text, meaning they were not born into serfdom. However, the tenements they held were subject to all the obligations of bondage, and these are spelled out in great detail in the extents.[50] Whether these free persons with bonded tenancies and associated services should be described as villeins (*villani*) is a debatable point. The discussion centres on the role of the common law and how, by the end of the twelfth century, those who held bonded tenancies were classed as being in serfdom by tenure. By contrast, those who were described as *nativi* or *nativa* had been born into serfdom.[51] In the Canonsleigh extents, the term *villanus/villana* is never applied to any individual. There are five examples of the use of the term 'of the villeins' (*villanorum*), but that is used as a general term encompassing both those called *nativi* and those called *liber corpore*.[52]

A clear example of serfdom is in the extent for the manor of Netherton – it provides a very full list of the obligations for John Pouke, serf of the lady abbess (*nativus domine*), on fol. 141r. On that same folio are found the names of Henry Pouke, John atte Hurne and John Matheu; all are described as having similar labour obligations as John Pouke even though they are free, not in bondage.[53] These three (and other similar tenants) are also subject to an additional levy (the *auxilium*, also known as tallage).[54] Later in the Netherton extent, the total value is described as *summa auxilii villanorum ibidem* (the total *auxilium* of the villeins there). Clearly, this additional tax burden is seen as one borne only by the unfree.[55]

The other group of tenants normally regarded as subject to villeinage are those who hold a *cotagium* (the cottagers, unfree smallholders, also known as cottars), who number forty. If we take them together with the villeins and the customary tenants,

---

[49] *Cartulary*, p. xv.

[50] That a freeman might hold villein land but not be personally servile was something seen more widely (see Baily, *The Decline of Serfdom*, pp. 17, 57).

[51] Phillipp R. Schofield, *Peasant and Community in Medieval England, 1200–1500*, Medieval Culture and Society, 1st edn (Palgrave Macmillan, 2002), pp. 12–13, doi:10.1057/9780230802711.

[52] *Villanorum* can be found within the manors of Dunsford (fol. 147r), Sheddon (fol. 153v), Netherton (fols 142r and 142v) and Rockbeare (fol. 144v).

[53] John atte Hurne is excused two of the four annual carrying services.

[54] The *auxilium* (aid) was 'an extraordinary tax paid once a year and distinguished from ordinary rent. It appears as a direct consequence of the political subjection of the tenantry: it is, in fact, merely an expression of the right to tallage' (Vinogradoff, *Villainage*, p. 293).

[55] The *auxilium* or *tallagium* (tallage) became one of the most important tests of villeinage under the common law (Bailey, *The Decline of Serfdom*, p. 47).

Table 8. The composition of Canonsleigh's tenantry.

Manor	Free tenants on free tenements	Free tenants on bonded tenements	Free tenants at will	Cottagers	Serfs	Total tenants	Percent serfs
Leigh	36	18	7	0	16	77	21
Rockbeare	4	8	0	8	2	22	9
Netherton	6	7	0	11	1	25	4
Dunsford	11	2	0	11	15	39	38
Hockford Waters	1	2	1	7	12	23	52
Northleigh	1	3	0	1	1	6	17
Sampford Arundel	3	0	1	0	0	4	0
Gusford	20	5	0	2	5	32	16
Sheddon	33	1	0	0	2	36	6
Manningtree	92	0	0	0	0	92	0
TOTALS	**207**	**46**	**9**	**40**	**54**	**356**	**15**

then we achieve 140 out of the total of 356, thus 39 per cent. London's estimate that around two-thirds of the tenantry were free is therefore in rough agreement.

The burdensome labour services of John Pouke in the manor of Netherton merit closer consideration because they illustrate the sorts of obligations placed upon medieval serfs. They would have been carried out on the abbey's demesne land within the manor and are described in the following table. These services were of significant value to the manorial lady, but to the serf they were a burden that would lessen and eventually be lifted, in particular in the decades after the Black Death.

Table 9. The labour services of John Pouke, serf, of Netherton.[56]

Type of service	Value to the lady abbess	Note
Ploughing half an acre for the winter crop		
Ploughing half an acre for the spring-sown crop		
Harrowing without food associated with the above	6½d. (for this together with the preceding two services)	'Without food', meaning the abbess will not provide it
Ploughing for one day in winter and another day in Lent	6d.	He will have dinner once in the day if he has beasts/oxen
Harrowing once in winter at the will of the lady abbess		And he will have dinner
Harrowing once in summer at the will of the lady abbess	1d. for this and the preceding service	And he will have dinner if he has draft animals
Harrowing half an acre, as is the custom, without food	½d.	
Mowing one acre of meadow without food	3d.	
Making hay for two days with one man	¾d.	
Drawing the hay or assisting with the hay ricks without food for half a day	½d.	
Reaping twelve acres without food	3s.	

---

[56] Pouke held one furlong of land at Poukehegh' for which he paid an annual rent of 3 shillings. He also owed an *auxilium* (aid or tallage) of 2 shillings and a penny (fol. 141r).

Performing four sessions of boon-reaping with one man with food twice in the day	5*d.*	
Providing four carrying services with one man and his own draught animal per year	6*d.*	To such a distance that he can still return home by the next day. When he comes to Leigh, he will have food
Performing a service for half a day in any forty weeks of the year	20*d.*	Each half day of the forty is worth ½*d.* No food is provided
Providing a carrying service for the millstone together with his neighbours	7*s* 1¼*d.*	The abbess will provide the wagon and two oxen with one servant
Cleaning the mill-pond or mill-leat (*bedum*) with his neighbours when the lady abbess so wishes	¾*d.*	Here the term *bedum* may refer more specifically to the mill-leat

If Pouke's burden appears heavy, his obligations pale against those of Stephen le Taillur of Compton Dundon in Somerset. The extent for that manor was compiled in 1287, and the printed edition spends four pages itemising le Taillur's lengthy list of works and services.[57] Some other restrictions or obligations were placed upon the bonded tenantry. At Netherton, the extent pronounces as follows (fol. 141v):

- Any bondsman will be the reeve if so elected. As reeve he will be quit (free) of all rents and services that he normally owes.
- Without the permission of the lady abbess he cannot do the following:
    - Have his sons educated (*ponere ad literaturam*)
    - Arrange marriage for his daughter
    - Sell a young male horse that has been foaled to him
    - Sell an ox that has been calved to him.

---

[57] *Two Registers Formerly Belonging to the Family of Beauchamp of Hatch*, ed. by H. C. Maxwell-Lyte, Somerset Record Society, 35 (Somerset Record Society, 1920), pp. 33–7. The manor of Compton Dundon was held of Glastonbury Abbey by knight service (M. C. Siraut, A. T. Thacker and Elizabeth Williamson, 'Parishes: Compton Dundon', in *A History of the County of Somerset: Volume 9, Glastonbury and Street*, ed. R. W. Dunning (Victoria County History, 2006), British History Online https://www.british-history.ac.uk/vch/som/vol9/pp103-120 [accessed 10 Nov. 2024]).

The stipulations concerning the sale of the male horse or ox can be seen in other manors, for example in Sussex.[58] The limitation on marriage of a daughter can also be found elsewhere.[59] A licence for education or apprenticeship was considerably rarer.[60] There is some evidence of tenants who may have agreed to pay additional rent in lieu of labour services. In the manor of Netherton (fol. 142r), there are names such as William atte Hurne, John Faber [Smith] and Matilda Turnour, where they pay rent that provides for all their services (*pro omnibus serviciis*). Unfortunately, the court rolls for 1323 – or for any part of the fourteenth century – do not survive for any of Canonsleigh's Devon manors. Thus we cannot trace any changes in Canonsleigh's tenancy agreements for this period.[61] For a tenant to provide a money payment in lieu of services was certainly not uncommon in the late medieval period. Campbell has estimated that commutation of villein labour services was so commonplace that only around one-half of all labour services were used in early fourteenth-century England.[62]

The Manors – Devon and Somerset

The abbey's western possessions are displayed on Map 2. The Somerset manor of Thorne St Margaret is not displayed as its income was itemised within the extent for the home manor of Leigh.

The Home Manor of Leigh

The longest single entry in the extents is for Canonsleigh's home manor of Leigh. It comprises eight and a half leaves or folios from fol. 167r to fol. 175r. The extent was surveyed on Sunday, 12 June 1323, and the entry opens with a list of the eleven jurors. Three of the jurors are subsequently named as being villeins.

A full description of the demesne land then follows under six categories (these are denoted in the left margin). The categories are arable land, meadow, moorland, woodland, waste land and finally the collective heading of gardens (or orchards), dovecote and mill. The 245-acre demesne at Canonsleigh was dispersed as blocks in several furlongs.[63] In addition there is a brief note concerning the value of the

---

[58] *Custumals of the Manors of Laughton, Willingdon, and Goring*, ed. by A. E. Wilson, Sussex Record Society Publications, 60 (Sussex Record Society, 1961), p. 71.

[59] F. M. Powicke, review of *Curia Regis Rolls of the Reigns of Richard I and John, Preserved in the Public Record Office. Vol. i, Richard I–2 John*, by C. T. Flower, *The English Historical Review*, 39, no. 154 (1924), pp. 264–72 (p. 269). Where the right to marriage was granted, this would typically incur the payment of merchet (Harvey, *Manorial Records*, p. 45); a standard tariff elsewhere in Devon for merchet was 1s. 3d. (Finberg, *Tavistock Abbey*, pp. 77–8).

[60] Bailey, *The Decline of Serfdom*, p. 46. No lord would wish to lose a source of labour from their manor, at least not without adequate compensation by way of a monetary fee.

[61] The only fourteenth-century court rolls that survive for any of Canonsleigh's manors are for the parish of Mistley, Essex (the manor of Sheddon and the borough of Manningtree). They are for the years 1317–29 and 1365–72 (TNA, SC 2/171/59) and are listed in the National Archives' Manorial Documents Register (https://discovery.nationalarchives.gov.uk/manor-search).

[62] Bailey, *Medieval Suffolk*, p. 54.

[63] W. G. Hoskins and H. P. R. Finberg, *Devonshire Studies* (Cape, 1952), p. 274. David Hall, *The Open Fields of England*, Medieval History and Archaeology, 1st edn (Oxford University Press, 2014), p. 98, doi:10.1093/acprof:oso/9780198702955.001.0001.

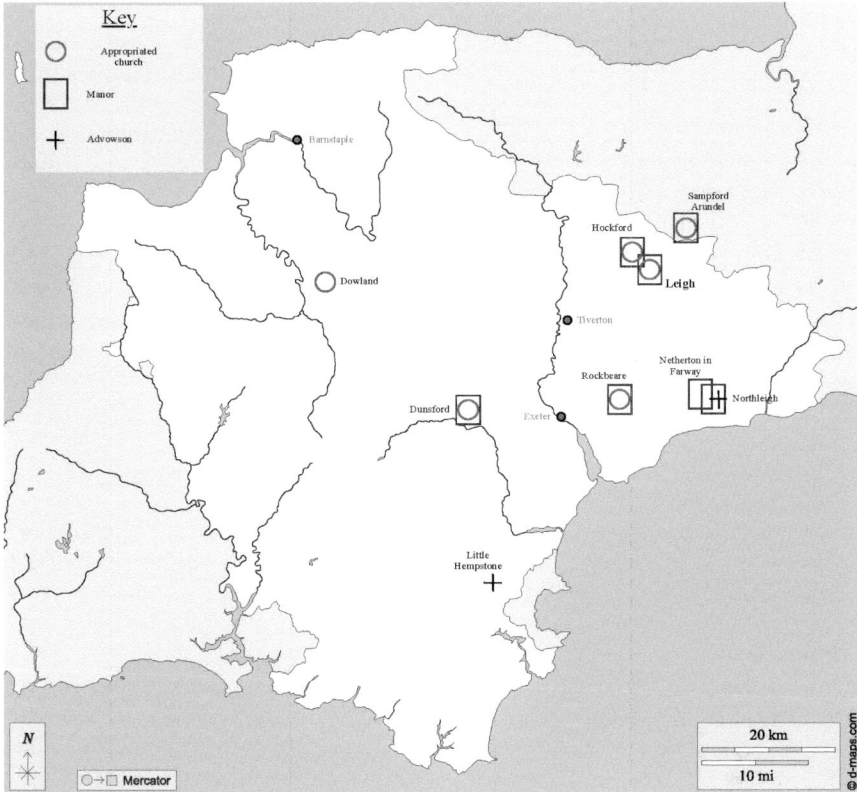

Map 2. Canonsleigh's possessions in Devon and Somerset.

church of Burlescombe, which was appropriated to the abbey. The annual value of the demesne plus the church is given as £14 0s 7½d. There then follows a description of the demesne land in the manor of Thorne St Margaret in Somerset. Although the extent does not separately provide a total value for Thorne, the individual figures add up to just under £2. Thus the total value of the two demesnes plus the church of Burlescombe is £16 0s 5d.

Next comes a list of fixed rents from three lords, John de Clavile, John de Aysforde and Hugh de Raleghe. They held nothing from the abbey but granted those rents to the abbey through their charters.[64] The total value to Canonsleigh was 31s.

There then follows a list of free tenants whose rents total £9 6s 5d by value. A total of thirty-six names, either of individuals or of groups of heirs (twelve in total), are listed. These include the abbot of Dunkeswell, who held land up on Exmoor at Challacombe (Schallecumbe) to the north-east of Barnstaple. One payment (from the heirs of William de Crues) was not in the form of money but of a pound of wax, due on or within the octave of Michaelmas (29 September).

---

[64] A charter (*carta* in Latin) was a legal document whereby a donor granted land or other privileges. They were often copied so that holders of land could provide evidence of their right to the property, and frequently what survives are these copies. The modern equivalent is the deed. Charters are a very valuable source of historical information.

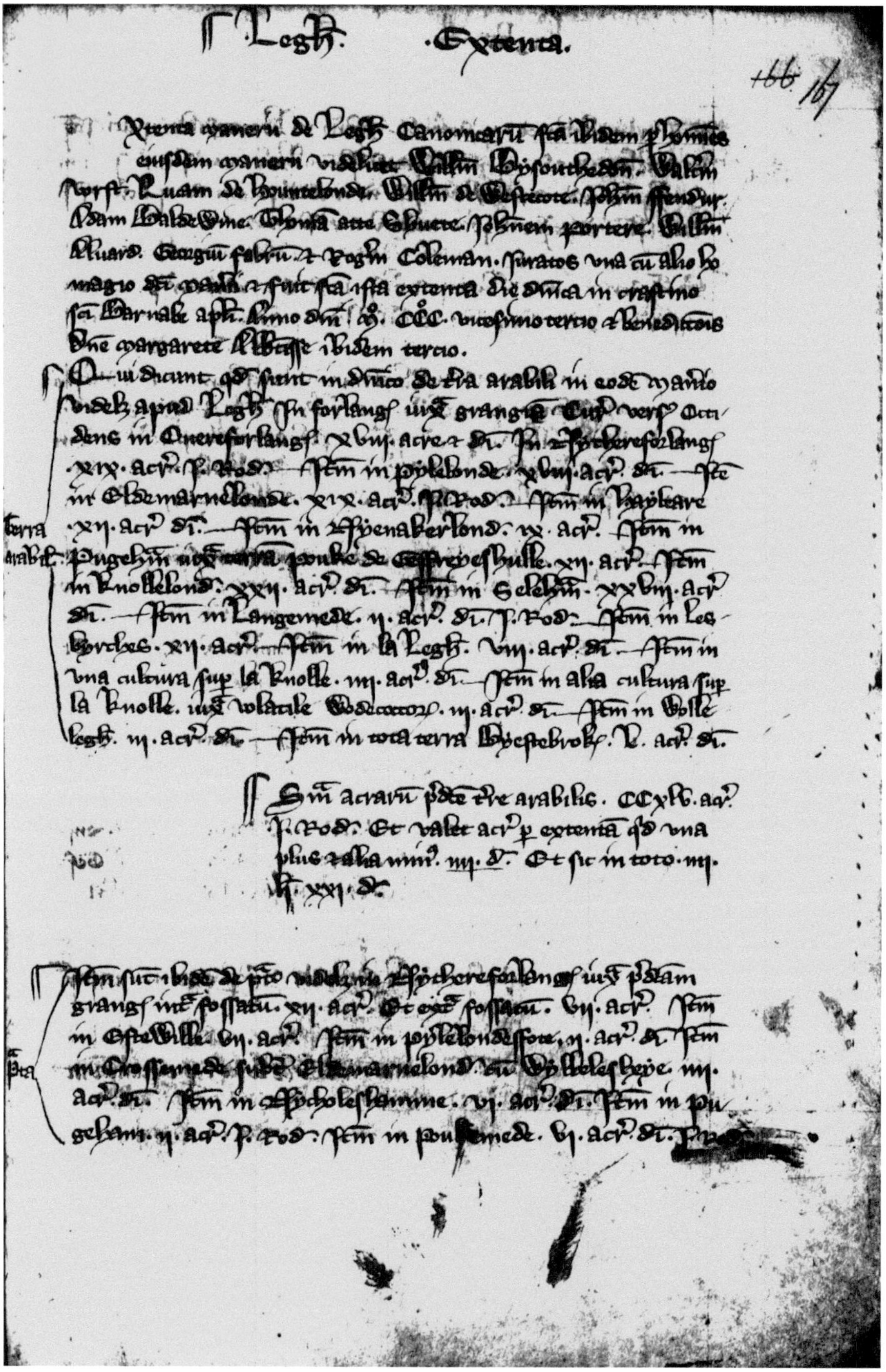

Fig. 5. The opening folio of the extent for the manor of Leigh, BL Harleian MS 3660, fol. 167r.

Three mills are mentioned. The first was at Pugham (Pugeham) to the south-west of Burlescombe. The tenant was John the miller, who held it for the term of his life as well as 3 acres of land. The annual rent he owed was 2 shillings.

The second mill was held by John Pistor, located at Knaphille (Knappemulle) just to the north-east of the abbey precinct. He paid 12 shillings per annum and held it at will (*ad voluntatem*) rather than by charter. Hence the abbess could freely grant the property to another tenant if she chose to do so. Pistor was responsible for the mill's general care and upkeep, except that the abbess would provide any timber needed to maintain the building plus the millstones and would provide for their carriage to the mill.

The third mill, located at Withycombe Raleigh (Wydecumbe), was in the hands of Lord Hugh de Courtenay. He paid 12 shillings per annum for the mill and 6 acres of land.

Fols 171r to 174v contain the names of thirty-six individuals who are described as being in bondage at will (*in bondagio ad voluntatem*). Many of these tenants are not villeins, however (i.e. they are not described as *nativus/nativa dominarum*). For example, Alice Atteslade and Robert de Pugeham (fol. 171v) are described as being free in body (*liber corpore*). They are holders of bonded tenancies and are required to carry out numerous services. Neither are required to pay aid/tallage in addition to their rents.[65] However, other free tenants on bonded tenancies (such as Richard de Goldemore on fol. 172r) were under that obligation. Walter Vorst, one of the jurors named at the beginning of the extent, is also required to pay tallage as well as the liability of being elected as reeve (fols 172v to 173r).

The total rent for the tenants in bondage or holding such tenancies at will is £6 11s 10d. In addition, their total liability for aid/tallage (*auxilium*) amounts to 20s 4¼d. There is also a minor liability to pay 5d as hearth-penny (hertselver or hertpeni), an annual tax levied on a very few of Leigh's householders. Although the surveyor appears to have had the intention of providing a valuation of the labour services of the tenants (*summa valoris operum*), he did not complete his entry on fol. 174v. The same is true for the value of their plough-service (*summa arature*). The total of all rents given on fol. 175r is £17 9s 3d plus 1 pound of wax. That total figure is followed by a memorandum concerning the liability to a heriot for the aforementioned tenants at will.[66] The extent ends by stating that if such a tenant should die or give up their tenancy, then there would be a liability as heriot of the best beast. Furthermore, if that tenant was of the parish of Burlescombe then the second best beast would be due as a mortuary payment (*mortuarium*).

The total income as listed above for the manor can be summarised in Table 10 below:

---

[65] See the Glossary for a definition of these terms.
[66] A heriot was a death duty, normally the best beast, levied by the manorial lord or lady on the estate of a deceased tenant.

Table 10. The income for the manor of Canonsleigh.

Item	£	s	d	Percentage of total
Demesne of Leigh	11	0	7½	31.95
Demesne of Thorne St Margaret, Somerset	1	19	9½	5.76
Church of Burlescombe	3	0	0	8.69
Rents from the lords (fol. 169r)	1	11	0	4.49
Rents from the other free tenants	9	6	5	27
Rents from ten-ants in bondage/ at will	6	11	10	19.08
Aid/tallage (*auxilium*)	1	0	4¼	2.95
Hearth-penny	0	0	5	0.06
TOTAL income	**34**	**10**	**5¼**	

In the *Valor* entry for Canonsleigh dating from 1535, there is a separate section entitled Chilloman & SouthTawton, that is, for Chieflowman and South Tawton.[67] Canonsleigh did have possessions there in 1323 (see the index of placenames in *Cartulary* for details), but the extents do not contain a separate entry for them. There are several entries for Chieflowman (as Childelomene and Chyldelomene), but these are all found within this extent for Leigh (see fols 169r, 174r and 174v).

The Devon Manor of Rockbeare
The manor and settlement of Rockbeare lie 6 miles east north-east of the centre of Exeter. The village is located a little to south of the main London Road, providing a very good transport link westwards to Exeter or eastwards to Honiton some 14 miles distant. The land is generally low-lying with a network of streams running between areas of gently rising ground. The manor had been granted to the abbey by Matilda de Clare in a grant made within the period 1287–9. She had recently received it from Robert Burnell, bishop of Bath and Wells. The overlord to both of them was Hugh de Courtenay – he licensed the countess to enfeoff the abbess and convent in July 1287.[68]

The extent for the manor of Rockbeare was surveyed on Tuesday, 28 June 1323, the information being provided by six male jurors. Of those, two were villeins, three

---

[67] *Valor*, ii, p. 329.
[68] See the *Cartulary*, items 262–5.

were freemen occupying bonded tenancies and one was a cottar. There are three tenants on free tenements listed in the extent, but none of them acted as juror.

Table 11. The demesne land of the manor of Rockbeare.

Category of demesne land	Size	Value	Value per acre
Arable	202 acres 1 perch	33*s* 8½*d*	2*d*
Meadows (*prata*) in Estparke and Westparke	41 acres	41*s*	1*s*
Other land, including the court and its close	4 acres	2*s*	6*d*
Woodland	27 acres	4*s* 6*d*	2*d*
Totals	**274 acres 1 perch**	**£4 1*s* 2½*d***	

The rental income exceeded the value of the demesne and is listed in Table 12 below.

Table 12. The income from rents and services at Rockbeare.

Item	Value	Notes
From free tenants on free tenements	14*s* 8*d*	Three males
From villeins and freemen on bonded tenancies	73*s* 8*d*	Fourteen males and four females
Services from the bonded tenants	18*s* 2½*d*	
Total rental income	**£5 6*s* 6½*d***	

Thus the manor's total gross income as revealed by the extent was £9 7*s* 9*d*. There is no information provided about income from the manorial court. That is puzzling as, by 1535, income listed as perquisites of the court, as well as from the pannage of pigs, the sale of woodland and so on is given as £12 10*s* 9*d*. Furthermore, the demesne lands themselves appear to have been leased out by then with a very healthy annual income of £7 0*s* 17*d*.[69]

There is no mention in the extent of income from the mill, although two of the bonded tenants were required to assist with the cleaning of its mill-dam or leat.[70] One curious entry relating to the mill can be found on fol. 143v. The villein (*nativus*) William atte Wille was required with others of his neighbours to carry the millstone there, and the recipient is described as the second purchaser (*secondo emptori*). Quite what that means is unclear – on fol. 143v, in the extent for the manor of

[69] *Valor*, ii, p. 328.
[70] Robert in the Toune and Alice Atteroke on fol. 144v.

Netherton, the villein John Pouke was required to carry the millstone to the third purchaser (*tercio emptori*). This query concerning mills is discussed at more length towards the end of this introduction. At Netherton, the extent does include income from the mill, but, as stated above, there is no such entry for Rockbeare.

The extent then goes on to provide several notes/memoranda, including the fact that Rockbeare manor owed suit of court at the hundred court of Ryngeswille, which was normally bought off for 4 shillings (i.e. it avoided having to attend by payment of a fee). The total net income of the manor was therefore £9 3s 9d.

The abbey held the advowson for the parish church of Rockbeare, but the church was not appropriated to Canonsleigh until 1333.[71] Thus no profit was accrued within the extent. The rector is listed as Master Gilbert Bydeford, and he may be the same man who had granted a property to Exeter College at Oxford in June 1303.[72] The living had been valued at £5 per annum in 1291.[73] By 1535, the value accruing to the abbey was £7 3s 4d.[74]

The final entries in the extent are four homages made by tenants to future abbesses during the fifteenth century.[75]

The Devon Manor of Dunsford

The manor and village of Dunsford lie around 6 miles to the west of Exeter and some 25 miles from the abbey. The village is located to the north of the River Teign and sits on higher ground that slopes gently up from the valley below. The exact date for the descent of the manor to the abbess and convent is not clear.[76] Dunsford had not been one of the possessions of the canons before the suppression of the priory. In 1276, the manor came into the possession of the bishop of Exeter, who must have granted it to Maude de Clare by around 1290. That grant included the advowson of Dunsford church. At that point, the church itself was a possession of the bishop, but in 1314 he granted it to the nuns because they 'lacked resources even for their daily needs'.[77]

The extent for Dunsford was surveyed on Wednesday, 29 June 1323; it included income from both the manor and church. Six jurors were listed, four villeins and two freemen. The extent then continues with a list of thirty-nine tenants of the manor containing both free and bonded tenants. As illustrated previously, the proportion purely of serfs (*nativi*, of whom there were fifteen) to the total is 38 per cent. However, if the cottars and the two free tenants on bonded tenements are included, then the proportion of unfree tenancy rises steeply to 72 per cent. This is the highest proportion for any of Canonsleigh's manors.

The first three tenants listed are freemen who held their land by hereditary right (*iure hereditario*). Two of them owe no rent. The first, Henry de Moulysch',

---

[71] *Reg. Grandisson*, ii, pp. 698–9.

[72] *BRUO*, i, p. 185.

[73] See the online *Taxatio* database at https://www.dhi.ac.uk/taxatio/benkey?benkey=EX. EX.AY.16 [accessed 3 Nov. 2024].

[74] *Valor*, ii, p. 329.

[75] See fol. 145r.

[76] The details that follow are taken from *Cartulary*, p. xxx.

[77] *Cartulary*, item 276. Walter Stapledon was bishop of Exeter from 1308 to 1326. He was also twice treasurer of England under Edward II and died at the hands of a mob in the London uprising of 1326.

is obliged to attend the manorial court whenever it is held, and 'he will be the tithingman for the whole manor in perpetuity' (*et erit decennarius pro toto manerio imperpetuum*). The second, Alexander Feraunt, has the obligation of military service (although a separate payment of cash may perhaps have been accepted in lieu of that).[78] Other freemen such as William de la Forde do pay rent and hold their land, not by military service, but in free socage (*in libero socagio*), owing neither religious nor military service.[79]

One term used widely within the Dunsford extent as a measure of the size of tenant holdings was *ferlingus*. The great majority of the holdings were defined using that measure, varying from a half to 5 ferlings. In particular, the size of the arable land within the demesne was defined as 'one and a half ferlings of land containing 90 acres of arable land. And the acre is worth in total 1*d* per annum' (*sunt ibidem in dominico .j. ferlingus terre et dimidius continens .iiij.xx et .x. acre terre arabilis. Et valet acra per annum in toto .j.d*).[80] To describe a ferling and a half as containing 90 acres is exceptional. The extent for the manor of Netherton also uses the term, but there it appears to be for 7.5 acres or thereabouts, matching the way it has been described elsewhere.

In his Latin word list, Latham defines *ferdingus* or *ferlingus* as '"ferling" of land, quarter-virgate'.[81] The dates he quotes encompass the period of the Canonsleigh extents. Other authors agree with that characterisation.[82] Likewise, he provides an entry for *virgata* (p. 514), defining it as 'yardland, virgate, square-measure usually of 20 to 30 acres (¼ carrucate)'.[83] The carrucate he defines as 'usually from 80 to 120 acres' (p. 73). In the study of another Devon manor (at Branscombe in the east of the county), a similar definition of the ferling was described.[84] However, the ferling has also been seen as primarily a fiscal term and 'areally inexact'.[85] We do perhaps have to assume that, to the jurymen of Dunsford, 'ferling' had a local meaning that did not match its usage elsewhere.

The valuations for the various sources of income to the abbey are summarised in Table 13 below.

[78] There is an Alexander Feraunt listed in *DLS* on p. 52 at Melhuish Barton.

[79] Mark Bailey, *The English Manor, c. 1200–1500*, Manchester Medieval Sources Series (Manchester University Press, 2002), p. 27. There is a William de la Forde listed in *DLS* on p. 74 at South Molton.

[80] Fol. 147v.

[81] Latham, *Revised medieval Latin Word-List from British and Irish Sources*, p. 188.

[82] J. L. Fisher, *A Medieval Farming Glossary of Latin and English Words Taken Mainly from Essex Records* (National Council of Social Service for the Standing Conference for Local History, 1968), p. 13.

[83] As does Bailey, *The English Manor*, p. 246.

[84] John Torrance, 'Branscombe 1280–1340: An East Devon Manor before the Black Death', *The Devon Historian* 81 (2012), pp. 67–80 (p. 69). 'On many manors the biggest holdings were virgates (four ferlings, usually reckoned as 30 acres)'; 'a ferling would be either 7.5 or 8.75 acres'.

[85] R. A. Butlin, 'Some Terms Used in Agrarian History: A Glossary', *The Agricultural History Review* 9, no. 2 (1961), pp. 98–104 (p. 102). Torrance in his Branscombe study similarly described ferlings and carucates as 'fiscal units based on land productivity and might vary in area'.

Table 13. The income from the manor and church of Dunsford.

Item	Value per annum	Quantity	Unit value
Rent (from both free and bonded tenants)	£10 5s 2½d		
Marshland	14d	7 acres	2d per acre
Oak wood	2s	12 acres	2d per acre
Waste land	6d	6 acres	1d per acre
Sub-total	**£10 8s 10½d**		
Domain arable	7s 6d	90 acres	1d per acre
Meadow	3s	3 acres	12d per acre
Dovecot	12d		
Court & garden	2s		
The church of Dunsford	£8 0s 0d		Value shown as twelve marks
Sub-total	**£8 13s 6d**		
Rents due to the parsonage	20s 6d		
Value of the church, parsonage rents, demesne and meadow	£9 14s 0d		
Deductions	55s 4d[86]		
Total value of the manor and church	**£17 7s 6½d**		

As with the other manors, the surveyor includes various notes to describe obligations or features of the manorial system in this place. Thus all tenants listed up to the end of fol. 146v 'will be the reeves if they are elected'; the exception is one John Walsch', who holds his land only for the term of his life. Each tenant and cottar, if they have beasts (*averia*), will have to give their best beast as heriot when they die; that applies to serfs who have beasts even if they hold no land.

One special feature of this manor was the liberty it had from being fined for such things as breach of the assize of bread and ale. That liberty also included freedom from the raising of gallows and the use of the drowning-pool (punishment due to male and female felons respectively).[87]

---

[86] An annual pension of 53s 7d was owing to the cathedral church of Exeter. Two shillings were also owed annually to the hundred of Wonford to redeem the obligation for suit of court there.

[87] The ordeal or judgement of water (*juisam aquae*) is described in Henry II's Assize of Clarendon written in 1166 (items 2 and 12).

Also, as with other manors, some later notes in a different, more cursive hand have been added at the bottom of several folios detailing the giving of homage to the abbess by new tenants for their lands and tenements.

The Devon Manor of Hockford

The manor of Hockford (or Hockford Waters) was centred around the small village of Hockworthy, which lies 2.5 miles north-west of Canonsleigh. The landscape here is gently undulating, with several streams and remains today a quiet, rural corner of east Devon. The extent is dated Sunday, 19 June 1323 and opens with a list of thirteen jurors. Two of those were freemen and ten were villeins. The other juror, Richard Pope, does not feature elsewhere as a tenant, but there are several tenants who share his surname.

The extent is unfortunately incomplete, ending abruptly on fol. 150v before the details of the demesne lands were given. It does provide details for twenty-three tenants and summarises the income from rents, tallage, works and services as provided in the table that follows.

Table 14. The rental income for Hockford manor and the deductions that were applied.

Item	Value	Notes
Tenant rents	£4 14s 2d	of which 7s 2d was from the seven cottars
Tallage/auxilium	£1 0s 1d	of which 2¼d was from the cottars
Value of all works	£1 5s 3¾d	
Sub-total	£6 19s 6¾d	
Less deductions:		as shown on fol. 150r
To Henry Bernevile	4s	
To the sheriff's court	2¼d	
To the hundred court of Bampton	40d	
Sub-total	7s 6¼d	
Net value	£6 12s ½d	

It may be possible to estimate the value of the demesne land, even if we cannot piece together the acreages and other resources it contained. In 1535, there is an entry for the manor of Hockford in the *Valor Ecclesiasticus*.[88] It shows that the income from rents was £5 15s 5d and from the demesne it was £9 12s 4d (both figures before deductions), a ratio of 1 to 1.67. If we assume a similar ratio would have applied in 1323, then we can multiply the total rental income shown above (as the rents of £4 14s 2d) by 1.67. The result is £7 17s 3d. That would suggest a total net value for the manor of somewhere over £14 9s per annum. Another missing item is the church – it had been granted to the canons and was worth £2 19s 8d in the *Taxatio*.

---

[88] *Valor*, ii, p. 328.

The Devon Manor of Netherton

Netherton in the parish of Farway is located around 3.5 miles south south-east of Honiton and less than 6 miles from the coastal settlement of Beer. Canonsleigh is around 17 miles distant to the north north-west. The River Coly runs through the manor on its way to join the Axe near Colyford. It is a very rural spot, linked today by a network of small lanes. This manor provides a very interesting example of a rural Devon manor in 1323, with its list of significant labour services and so forth. For that reason, a full transcription and translation of the extent has been provided as Appendix 1. The reader will find a series of footnotes there that provide additional detail and background. The heavy labour services of the Netherton serf, John Pouke, have been discussed earlier.

When Canonsleigh Priory was founded as a house of Augustinian canons in the twelfth century, Netherton was one of its initial endowments. It remained in the abbey's possession until the Dissolution in 1539. The extent of 1323 was dated Monday, 27 June. It begins with the list of six jurors and then immediately summarises the landed possessions of the manor with acreages and values (drawn together in Table 15 below). One unusual feature is the binding up of this manor's extent within the manuscript. It begins on fols 178r and 178v, but the subsequent folios can be found at 141r to 142v inclusive. However, the foliation is not medieval; instead, there are two modern ones.[89]

Table 15. The valuations for the manor of Netherton.

Item	Value per annum	Quantity	Unit value
Demesne arable	33s 3d	133 acres	3d per acre
Waste land	3s	18 acres	2d per acre
Meadow	16s	17 acres[90]	12d per acre
Alder wood	21d	7 acres	3d per acre
The court and close	6d	2 acres	3d per acre
The common pasture	nil	60 acres	nil
The dovecot	12d	1	12d
The mill	24s	1	24s
Sub-total	*79s 6d*		
Total rents (both free and bonded tenants)	61s ½d		

---

[89] *Cartulary*, p. xxxiii.
[90] It is unclear why the scribe has written 17 acres here. There are 18 acres of meadow but two are described as not mown and so should be excluded. Thus the annual value of 16s would be correct for the 16 mown acres. To be precise, the list of meadows amounts to 16 acres and 4 perches, plus the two that are not mown.

Income from tallage	12*s*
Income from labour services	34*s* 8*d*
Gross total value	£9 7*s* 2 ½*d*
less deductions	4*s* 5*d*
Net total value	**£9 2*s* 7½*d***

Having provided details of the demesne land, its values and other features, the extent then goes on to list the twenty-five tenants, their holdings and obligations. Six were free tenants with no labour obligations. Seven other free tenants occupied bonded tenements and therefore owed labour services and/or tallage (*auxilium*). Only one tenant, John Pouke, is explicitly described as a serf of the lady (*nativus Domine*). The other eleven tenants were cottars.

The three 'open' fields in the extent for Netherton (fol. 178r) are modest in size (Estfeld 45 acres, Myddelfeld 44 acres, Westfeld 45 acres). They do not compare with the open field sizes of central England of several hundred acres. In Devon, much larger fields can be found elsewhere, such as Braunton Great Field with its 350 acres.[91] Those at Netherton are, however, those of the demesne itself – they are not the shared fields of the tenantry. Smaller still are the fields within the demesne at Northleigh: 11.5 acres in the south field (*Campo Australi*), 15 acres in Middelfeld and 14 acres in Northfeld. None of the other manors have fields of this type within the demesne land.

The Somerset Manor of Sampford Arundel
Sampford Arundel lies immediately across the Devon/Somerset border less than 3 miles from Canonsleigh. The northern part of the manor includes damp, low-lying ground that slopes down towards the Westford Stream. The southern part rises up on to the slopes of the Blackdown Hills. This was a small manor, providing only a modest income to the abbey. Of particular interest from this extent is perhaps the earliest known reference to the name Blackdown (*Blakedoune* on fol. 175v) for the hills to the south of the manor. Another local name that persists to the present day is Beambridge (*Bembrygge*, same folio).

The extent was surveyed on Sunday, 12 June 1323, the same day as that for the home manor of Leigh. No jurors are listed (there are only three tenants described in the extent). The possessions on the demesne are listed first, followed by details of the appropriation of the church. Next the mill is itemised – it was held at farm by a Benedict Collebon for the sum of 10 shillings per annum. A full description of the conditions attached to that arrangement were provided by London.[92]

The tenant Roger Frankeleyn held his tenement at will. The other two tenants listed appear to have held theirs in freedom. The holdings are small. By far the most

---

[91] David Hall, *The Open Fields of England, Medieval History and Archaeology*, 1st edn (Oxford University Press, 2014), pp. 245–6, doi:10.1093/acprof:oso/9780198702955.001.0001; W. G. Hoskins and H. P. R. Finberg, *Devonshire Studies* (Cape, 1952), p. 265.
[92] *Cartulary*, item 123 (with London's note).

sizeable income was from the church of Sampford – 7 marks or 93s 4d.[93] Two other names are mentioned in relation to the provisions for the support of the perpetual vicar: neither Stephen de Bosco nor Thomas de la Doune are itemised among the list of tenants, but their meadows are mentioned earlier in the *Cartulary*.[94] The date of that item is 1251, so the individuals named there (including what must be an earlier Roger Frankeleyn) would surely have been long dead by the time of the extents.

Table 16. The holdings and income for Sampford Arundel.

Item	Value per annum	Quantity	Unit value
Demesne arable	21s 5d	64 acres	4d per acre
Moorland	17d	4 acres 1 rod	4d per acre
The church	7 marks (93s 4d)		
The mill (held at farm)	10s		
Tenant rents	52d		
Total income	**£6 10s 6d**		

The small income from tenant rents reflects the size of their holdings (2 acres plus a croft and a curtilage). Some further land was clearly held by the abbey since the abbess was described as holding 'two messuages and one hundred acres of land in the township' in a legal case brought in 1347.[95]

That the abbess was not the lady of the manor is clear from various sources beyond the extents. Until around 1260, the lordship was in the hands of John Arundel, son of Nicholas Arundel.[96] John had no male heirs, and so the manor was divided between his two daughters, Arundela (who was married to Richard Crispin) and Joan (married to John Paz). When Joan died without heirs, the whole reverted to Arundela. The succeeding holders were William Crispin, her son, and Roger Crispin, her grandson. Roger's son, Thomas, succeeded his father, but the male line then failed, and his lands passed to Elizabeth Crispin, his sister.[97] She subsequently married Sir John Streech of Dorset, who was seized of the manor (by right of his wife) until his death in September 1355. Elizabeth died less than two months later.[98]

Thus, at the time the extent was produced in June 1323, the manor was held by members of the Crispin family. Canonsleigh's temporal holding was a modest one. A much clearer picture of the total value of the manor's temporal possessions emerges in the reign of Henry IV. An extent produced in either 1405 or 1406 shows that the lord (then Sir Hugh Luttrell) had an income valued at £12 6s ½d from rents and services. That extent provides the names and rents of nine free tenants, thirteen

[93] A mark was worth two-thirds of a pound, i.e. 13s 4d (160 pence).
[94] *Cartulary*, item 119.
[95] *Cartulary*, App. 1, item XI.
[96] *Cartulary*, item 127 where John Arundel is called 'lord of Sandford'.
[97] Elizabeth was the great-great-granddaughter of Sir John Arundel, who, as described above, had died in 1260.
[98] See *Cartulary*, pp. xxiv–xxv for further details.

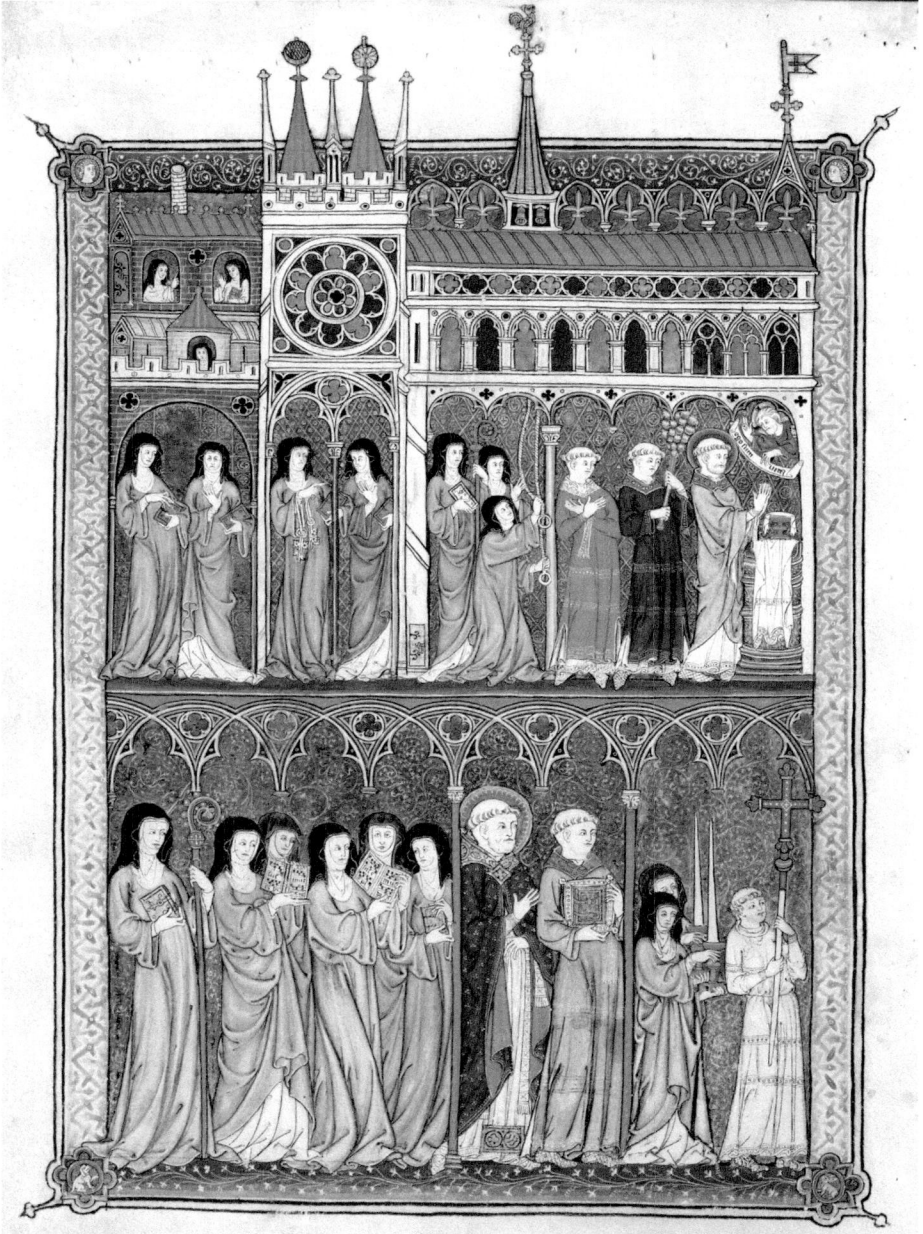

Fig. 6. A nunnery procession and mass, BL Yates Thompson II, fol. 6v; Northern France, *c*. 1290.

villeins, eight cottars and thirteen customary tenants. An accompanying annual account shows a total annual income of £20 6s 3d.[99] Against those figures, the rental income to the abbey in 1323 of just 52d looks very modest. By 1535, that had grown to 54s 4d.[100]

The extent ends with a memorandum describing the provision of the perpetual vicarage, repeating what had been laid down in the ordinance of the bishop in 1251 to Canonsleigh Priory and its canons. Church offerings, a proportion of the tithes and various agricultural produce are itemised. In return, the vicar was responsible for serving the church itself, with all other burdens falling on the canons.[101]

The Devon Manor of Northleigh

The manor of Northleigh lies just to the east of Netherton. The River Coly flows through the undulating landscape of this part of east Devon.[102] What was exceptional about the manor was that it was a net drain on the abbey's finances. As can be seen from Table 17 below, the extent recorded a debit of over 13s. By the time of the *Valor Ecclesiasticus* in 1535, the manor was no longer recorded as one of Canonsleigh's possessions. It seems clear that the abbey still had possession in 1396.[103] However, the manor was incorporated by Henry IV (reigned 1399 to 1413) into the Duchy of Lancaster.[104] In 1481, there are letters describing the seisin of the manor and the advowson of the church at Northleigh as belonging to several named laymen.[105]

In 1323, the demesne was relatively modest in size, with a total value of 19s. Only six tenants are listed, yielding just less than 27s in rent, tallage and services. That total income of almost 46s was more than swallowed up by the outgoings due to Nicholas de Mortesthorne (19s 1d for the term of his life) and Lady Petronilla de Kareute (40s for the term of her life).[106] There was no income from the church at Northleigh for which Canonsleigh held a moiety of the advowson.[107] The grant of Northleigh had been made by Matilda de Clare's grandson in 1314, and it was for just the half-portion of the manor that the countess had purchased in 1284–8.[108] Given the size of the outgoings, it was perhaps no surprise that the abbey might seek to relinquish its tenure.

---

[99] SHC, DD/L/P.1/14.

[100] *Valor*, ii, p. 329.

[101] Those provisions appear on fol. 176r of the extents and are also found in fol. 65r of the cartulary (*Cartulary*, item 119).

[102] 'Northleigh lies remote among the among the luxuriant valley scenery of East Devon' (W. G. Hoskins, *Devon* (Phillimore, 2003), p. 445).

[103] DHC, 123M/TB/365–6.

[104] *Cartulary*, p. xxx.

[105] DHC, 123M/TB/499.

[106] In 1288, Nicholas de Mortesthorne (Mosterton) had granted his possessions in the manor of Northleigh to Matilda de Clare (*Cartulary*, item 268). There is no mention there of an ongoing payment during his lifetime. However, if the same Nicholas was still alive in 1323, then the financial burden of a payment for life was perhaps more long-lived than the abbey might have expected. As regards Petronilla de Kareute, within the cartulary the only individual named Petronilla is the abbess Petronilla de Clare. There is no obvious reference to any similar surname in, for example, the inquisitions post mortem for the reign of Edward II.

[107] *Cartulary*, p. xv. A moiety is a share, typically a half-share.

[108] *Cartulary*, p. xxix.

Table 17. The income and deductions for the manor of Northleigh.

Item	Value per annum	Quantity	Unit value
Demesne arable	6s 9d	40 acres	2d per acre
Meadow	8s 6d	8.5 acres	12d per acre
Alder wood	2s	8 acres	3d per acre
Hoberdesmille (fol. 176v)	12d		
Broom-land	1d	1 acre	1d per acre
Court close	8d	1 acre	8d per acre
Sub-total	19s		
Total rents	16s 4d		
Sum of tallage	2s 3d		
Sum of services	8s 2¼d		
Sub-total	26s 9¼d		
Grand total income	45s 9¼d		
less deductions	59s 1d		
Net negative value	**-13s 3¾d**		

The brief extent for Northleigh is dated Monday, 27 June 1323. Four male jurors from among the tenantry are listed – the other two tenants were both female. A list of the demesne lands and resources is then followed by the details of the six tenants. The extent concludes with a statement giving details of the obligations to the two lifetime individuals named above followed by a description of the advowson.

At Northleigh and elsewhere, the proportion of tenants who were female was not high. Married women had no absolute right to hold land under the common law.[109] However, it was normally the custom of the manor for a widow to be granted access to any dower should her husband pre-decease her. That protection could be increased if the land were held jointly by the husband and wife. Some customs allowed the widow to keep the whole tenement for her life provided she did not re-marry.[110] By reason of inheritance, a woman might also be the sole holder of a parcel of land. In that circumstance, a marriage to her would be highly advantageous to any prospective husband. Indeed, the manorial authorities might even compel a single woman to marry, especially where a religious authority was the manorial lord. However, for the woman, marriage might result in loss of control of her land – an incentive to remain single.[111] For Canonsleigh's Devon manors, it is unfortunate that

[109] Bailey, *The English Manor*, p. 29.
[110] Edward Miller, *Medieval England: Rural Society and Economic Change, 1086–1348*, Social and Economic History of England, repr. with corrections (Longman, 1980), p. 135.
[111] S. H. Rigby, *English Society in the Later Middle Ages Class, Status and Gender* (Macmillan Education UK, 1995), pp. 256–57, 260, doi:10.1007/978-1-349-23969-6.

no court rolls are known to have survived for the period before the Black Death –
that is where decisions affecting landholding for the women of the manor would
have been recorded.

The Manors of the Eastern Counties

The Essex Manor of Sheddon

The two eastern manors itemised in the extents were Sheddon in Essex (including
the small town of Manningtree) and Gusford in Suffolk. They are illustrated on the
following map.

The table that follows provides a breakdown of the valuations for this manor.

Table 18. Canonsleigh's possessions in the manor of Sheddon.

Item	£	s	d
Rent of free tenants	3	12	1½
Rent from bonded tenements	0	5	6
Value of services and works	0	8	8¼
Sum of items farmed out	0	11	6
Value of arable land	8	10	4
Value of meadow	1	19	0
Value of pasture	0	3	8
Value of alder woodland	4	13	9
Perquisites of the court and customs of the market	4	6	8
Sub-total of annual value for Sheddon itself	**24**	**11**	**2¾**
Sum of rents for Manningtree	3	10	4¾
Sum of items farmed out in Manningtree	0	6	3
Sub-total of annual value for Manningtree	**3**	**16**	**7¾**
Combined total for Sheddon with Manningtree	**£28**	**7s**	**10½d**

The combined total shown in the table falls short by 11s 6d of the total given in the
extent on fol. 163v. There, the scribe has written £28 19s 4½d. However, he appears

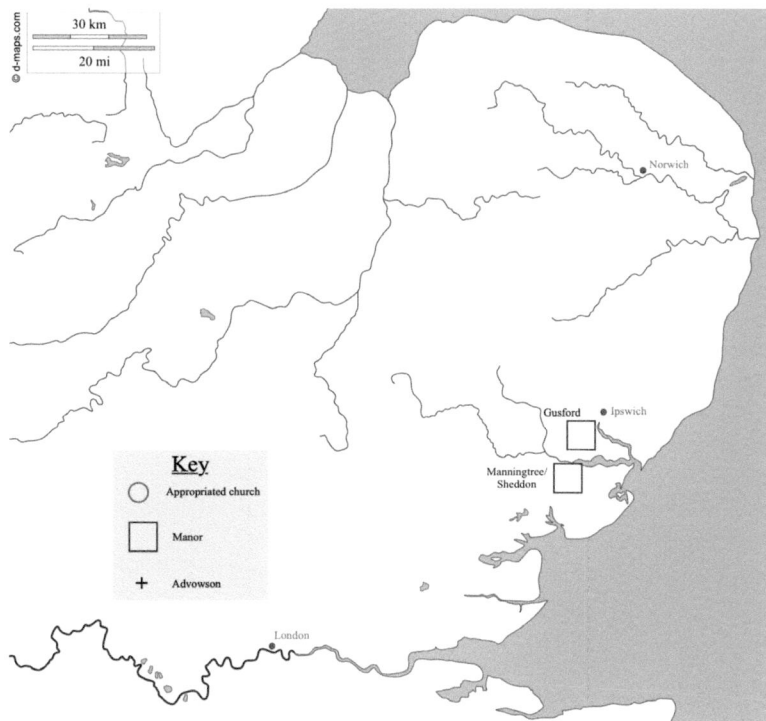

Map 3. The eastern possessions of Canonsleigh.

to have counted the income from the farm in Sheddon twice, once in arriving at his total for Sheddon (fol. 153v) but then by adding it once again in the combined total for Sheddon and Manningtree.

The extent for Sheddon begins with the normal opening paragraph giving the date for the survey as Tuesday, 9 August 1323. However, the list of names of the jurors is omitted, and there is no indication of how many jurors took the oath. There then follows a list of twenty-seven free tenants whose rents total 72s 1½d. Next comes the short list of three bonded tenancies; one is held by a freeman and the other two by villeins. One of the villeins is Geoffrey the reeve. Their rents total 5s 6d, and their services are valued at 8s 8¼d. They were also obliged to hand over four hens and fifteen eggs.

There is a loss or decay of rent and services with a total value of 17s (fol. 153v).

A list of the items held at farm and by whom then follows with a total value of 11s 6d. That total excludes the payment owing by Robert le Porter of 12s because the source or warrant of that payment is not known (*et nescitur quo Warento*).

At this point on fol. 153v, there is a memorandum stating that the measurement of the land, meadows and woodland is written after the extent for the manor of Gusford. Hence it is clear that the order of the folios had already been settled with that for Sheddon continuing on fol. 162v.

On fol. 162v, the measurement of the demesne acreages begins. This section opens with a new date of September 1323 (no specific day is given). Of the 255.5 acres of

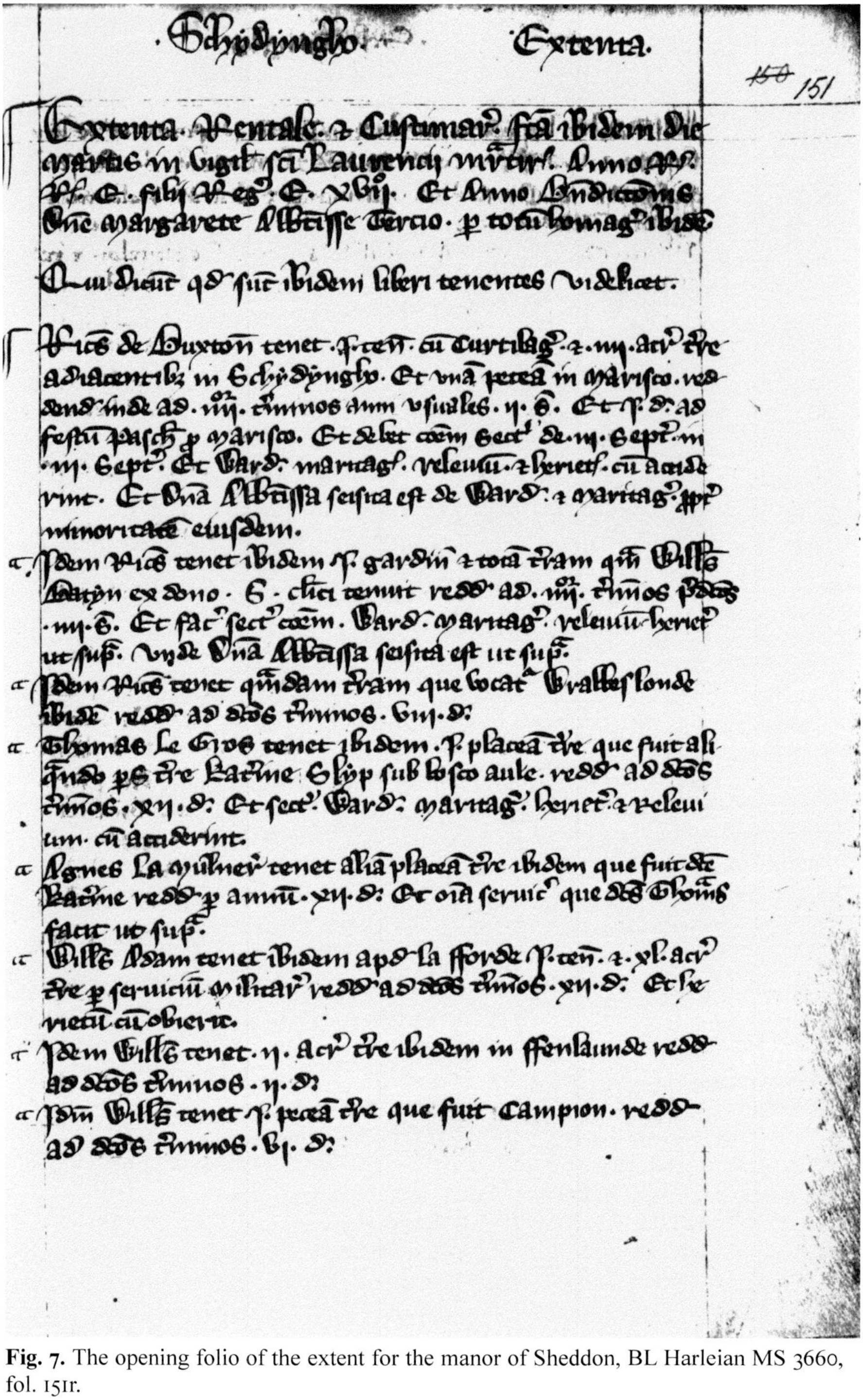

Fig. 7. The opening folio of the extent for the manor of Sheddon, BL Harleian MS 3660, fol. 151r.

arable land, over 32 acres are listed in the left margin as fallow (*warectum*). The four tenements or fields concerned are named as Somenoreslond, Hocroft, Litelhocroft and Pyrifeld. Some of the sizings are very precise, going down to quarters of a perch. The folio opens by talking of *mensuratio terrarum*; this seems to imply that a real effort was made to measure the land areas rather than simply estimating them (the term *per estimationem* would surely have been used in that instance).

Table 19 that follows summarises the size of each type of land within the demesne with its value and size.

Table 19. The Sheddon demesne.

Category of demesne land	Size	Value	Value per acre
Arable	255.5 acres	£8 10s 4d	8d
Meadows (*prata*)	9 acres, 1 rod, 13 perches	39s	4s
Pasture	5.5 acres, 8.5 perches	3s 8d	8d
Alder wood	31 acres, 1 rod, 17 perches	£4 14s 9d	3s

The table illustrates how meadow and woodland were worth so much more per acre than arable or pasture. Although the alder wood was less than 32 acres in size, it was worth more than half the value of the 255.5 acres of arable land. The alder was clearly grown on wet ground as is shown by the locations described – all five are fens.

The extent concludes with some further totals. This is one of two direct references in the Canonsleigh extents to the perquisites of the court, that is, income derived from the manorial court.[112] The sum listed (£4 6s 8d) also includes something described as *consuetudinem marcatorum*, meaning 'of the customs of the merchants'. This may well have involved payments coming into the court as the result of mercantile activity at Manningtree with its quayside on the River Stour.

Some marshland is also described plus a defunct windmill 'consumed with age' (*vetustatem consumitur*), where the millstones were broken and no longer usable. Two fishponds extending across 4 acres provided no profit and were therefore not given any value in the extent. An earlier survey of the manor made in 1279 is also available.[113] The comparative figures for this extent compared to those for 1323 are given in Table 20 below.

---

[112] At fol. 163v. The second reference is for the other eastern manor of Gusford at fol. 159r.

[113] TNA C 145/37 (Miscellaneous Inquisitions from 7 Edw. I). The extent was produced by the sheriff of Essex. Sheddon together with the Suffolk manor of Gusford had been held by the de Roylly family until around 1277 when Countess Maud de Clare took possession (ERO, T/P 61/1).

Table 20. Comparative numbers from the extents of 1279 and 1323.

Item description	1279 extent (TNA, C 145/37)	1323 extent (BL, Harley MS 3660)
Demesne arable (acres)	160	255.5
Demesne arable (value)	42s 6d	£8 10s 4d
Meadow and upland (acres)	7.5	9
Meadow and upland (value)	15s	£1 19s
Pasture (acres)	28	5.5
Pasture (value)	14s	3s 8d
Woodland (acres, under pasturage (*herbagio*) in 1279. Described as alder wood in 1323).	27	31
Woodland (value)	10s	£4 14s 9d
Water mill (value)	1 mark	Now defunct
Dovecote (value)	4s	2s (at farm)
Marsh (acres)	2	3
Marsh (value)	12d	24d
Assize rent and work of customary tenants	£7 6s 8d	£8 14s 5½d
Toll income	40s	Not listed

The discrepancy in the number of arable acres may be partially explained by over 32 acres being listed as fallow in 1323. The very large discrepancy in terms of value is more puzzling. In 1279, the arable land is valued at 3d per acre, whereas in 1323 the value is 8d. It seems inconceivable that agricultural improvement in just over forty years could lead to such an increase in value. A much broader study of land values across the first half of the fourteenth century suggests that a figure of 3d per acre was typical for this north-eastern part of Essex.[114] Across Canonsleigh's other manors, none of the demesne arable was valued at more than 4d per acre (Leigh and Rockbeare). The surveyor's arithmetic is correct in that he divides the value of Sheddon's arable land (2,044 pence) by the acreage (255 and a half) to reach his value per acre of 8d. It seems likely therefore that the valuation itself is at fault.

---

[114] Bruce M. S. Campbell, *English Seigniorial Agriculture, 1250–1450*, Cambridge Studies in Historical Geography, 31 (Cambridge University Press, 2000), p. 351.

The Essex Town (burgus) of Manningtree

The extent for Manningtree was created on the same day as that for the manor of Sheddon, namely Tuesday, 9 August 1323. Just as with Sheddon, there is no list of names for the jurors. The extent is in two sections: first a list of tenants and their rents and second a brief list of the properties held at farm. The numbers of tenants and properties are summarised in Table 21 below. There is also one reference to a boundary ditch with water course held by John Dryuer' and Roger Fyne next to their messuage.[115]

Table 21. A summary of the numbers of tenants and of other items in Manningtree.

Item	Count	Notes
Number of tenements (*tenementa*) rented out	94	Fourteen of the holders were female
Number of tenants holding properties at farm (*ad firmam*)	6	All these properties are on fol. 158r
Number of shops (*schoppe*)	9	Four were held by females
Number of market stalls or shambles (*scamella*)	8	None were held by females
Number of plots/sites (*placee*)	13	Two of the holders were female
Number of houses	2	Held by two males

Manningtree was the one urban centre among Canonsleigh's holdings. It lies on the south bank of the River Stour where the river widens out significantly, flowing east towards Harwich and the North Sea. By the time the river has reached Manningtree, it is already tidal, and the extent describes one plot (*unam placeam*) as being next to the salt water (*iuxta aquam salsam*).[116] The town appears to have been planned and established as a port for the locality, probably a century before the Canonsleigh extent. The first known mention of Manningtree is in 1248, and only limited archaeological work has been undertaken in the medieval core of the town. However, it may be that waterside and quayside features could be revealed in future work.[117] Such work could confirm the information provided in the grant of May 1540, where Henry VIII provided to John Raynforth of Bradfield, knight, the manors of Manningtree/Sheddon and Gusford.[118] Here we find the following details itemised: 'le Crane, le Key and Keyhouse in Manytree'.[119]

A chapel is mentioned in the *Cartulary* where a plot of land was granted to Roger Fyne and his wife Margery; the tenement of Thomas Alfeld (Alfeld in the extent)

---

[115] Fol. 155r.

[116] The plot of Walter Somenour, fol. 157v. The *Cartulary* also talks of the saltwater river of Manitre (p. 86, item 232),

[117] See the Tendring District Historic Environment Characterisation Project (2008), pp. 74–7: https://legacy.tendringdc.gov.uk/sites/default/files/documents/planning/Planning_Policy /S2Examination/Evidence/EB7.4.2%20TDC%20Historic%20Environment%20Charac terisation%20Report%202008.pdf [accessed 18 Oct. 2024].

[118] MUL, CRU/510.

[119] This detail comes from TNA's catalogue entry.

was described as being to the north.[120] The extent confirms this, showing that Roger
Fyne held tenements both to the north and south of that chapel (fol. 155r). There is no
further information concerning the chapel in 1323. However, by the much later reign
of Edward VI, there are records showing that it was dedicated to the Holy Trinity
and had a guild or fraternity of that name. The guild and chapel were granted out in
September 1550, and the entry in the roll provides a good level of detail:[121]

> Grant to the said John (Raynforth, knight) of ... the late chapel of Manytre
> in Manitre, the guild or fraternity of Manitre there and all buildings, lead and
> [p. 405] bells of that chapel, and the lands called le Chappel Yarde, Rouers-
> lande, le Swanne, Dochyns Holdynge, Pyllockes Feld, Androwes, Thewittes,
> le Pristes Chamber, Bakers Tenement, le Kynges Yarde, Bewfordes, Spornes
> Land, Asshelong, le Chappel Howse alias le Pristes Chamber and Widow
> Patenshows in Manytre or elsewhere which belonged to that chapel and
> guild, and also the lands in the several tenures of Thomas Rampston, William
> Cristmas, William Londesdale, Ralph Toothe, [John] Darnel, Nicholas
> Brickelbanke, Thomas Lytle, Henry Wormyngham, Henry Whyte, John
> Browne and Robert Dickey, gentleman, in Manytre or elsewhere, and all other
> possessions in Essex of the said chapel and guild.

We may assume that the eleven men named here are the members/stockholders
of the guild. That is a reduction from the sixteen men described in June 1481.[122] The
yearly value of the guild amounted to £8 5s 4d, and at the time of its suppression
its goods included a pair of organs, two hand bells, three chalices of silver and one
silver pax.[123] The chapel is described as being a mile and a quarter distant from the
parish church at Mistley. Just how much of this detail can be visited back upon
the chapel earlier in its life is very uncertain. However, it does seem likely that the
inhabitants of Manningtree in 1323 would similarly have wanted to display a strong
sense of local pride in their own religious centre.

Elsewhere in the Manningtree extent, we see the rector of Wrabness (*Wrabbenose*)
holding a tenement. He is named as John de Cottone.[124] The church of All Saints,
Wrabness was in the patronage of the powerful abbey of Bury, and Sir John de
Cottone was already rector there in 1308.[125]

There are several street names in the text. These include Cornhill Street (fol.
154r), Pleysaunte Lane (fol. 155r), Chapelle Street (fol. 155r) and Pernele Lane (fol.
156r). One notable building is 'la Tolhouse' (fol. 154r), which may have stood on the
current High Street. That street would have been the main Colchester to Harwich
road in this period and would have been the obvious location for a toll barrier.[126] The

---

[120] *Cartulary*, p. 88 (item 237).
[121] *CPR, Edward VI, Vol. 3, 1549–1551*, ed. by HMSO (HMSO, 1925), pp. 404–5.
[122] BL, Add. MS 15604.
[123] ERO, T/P 51/2, fol. 81.
[124] Fol. 157v.
[125] See https://archive.org/stream/threeroydonfamilooroyd/threeroydonfamilooroyd_djvu.txt
[accessed 3 Oct. 2024], quoting Harleian Charter 55, c.27.
[126] A. P. Baggs et al., 'Communications', in *A History of the County of Essex: Volume 9, the
Borough of Colchester*, ed. Janet Cooper and C. R. Elrington (Victoria County History, 1994),

extent of 1323 does not describe any income from a toll; however, there is a brief extent from 1279 that describes an annual toll income of 40*s* accrued to the manor of Sheddon.[127]

The workshop of the smith was next to la Tolhouse and was held by Robert the smith who owed 2*s* 6*d* for all services.[128] Another intriguing entry is that for Robert Munt (fol. 156r), whose tenement is given the name of 'La Werkhous'. At this period, it seems likely that this term refers to a place of industry or other activity rather than to an institution for poor relief. A bakehouse (*pistrina*) is mentioned as once being held by a Henry Caperoun (fol. 157r). By 1417, there is evidence for a schoolmaster resident in Manningtree, although Harley MS 3660 provides no information on that subject.[129]

One notable characteristic of the Manningtree extent is the numerous mentions of the name of an earlier holder of a tenement. In total, there are twenty-seven instances of this feature. Just why this was done is not clear. It might reveal that there had been a recent and quite widespread turnover of tenancies.[130] In that circumstance, the surveyor may have wanted to clarify which tenement he was discussing. Perhaps the name he found in the most recent record of the manorial court was that earlier name, and he therefore wanted to ensure that a link to the previous occupant of the tenement could be clearly established.

The Suffolk Manor of Gusford

The manor of Gusford (Guthelesford, Goddlesford) was located to the south-west of Ipswich in the county of Suffolk. It lies within the parish of Belstead. Gusford was one of the eastern possessions granted to Canonsleigh by Maud, countess of Gloucester, although the manor was not transferred to Canonsleigh by the time of her death in 1289. The abbey must have had possession by April 1309 as in that month it granted half an acre of land and a house in Gusford to Robert Scot and his wife.[131] The Manorial Documents Register of the TNA contains no documents for this manor before the year 1600.[132] Unlike the manor of Sheddon, Gusford was an entirely rural possession in 1323. In modern times, it has been absorbed within the town and borough of Ipswich. The values and acreages of the holdings and other items are given in Table 22 below.

British History Online, https://www.british-history.ac.uk/vch/essex/vol9/pp233-237 [accessed 4 Oct. 2024], p. 233.

[127] TNA, C 145/37.

[128] Fol. 158r.

[129] ERO, T/P 51/2 fol. 45 states that Magister William Haddeman, 'scholemeister de Manyngtre', is mentioned in the will of John Wallis, dated 1417.

[130] Well before the Black Death 'extensive geographical mobility had already become an integral experience of country life in Essex' – L. R. Poos, *A Rural Society after the Black Death: Essex 1350–1525*, Cambridge Studies in Population, Economy, and Society in Past Time, 18 (Cambridge University Press, 1991), p. 160, doi:10.1017/CBO9780511522437.

[131] *Cartulary*, 236 (p. 88). The names of Robert Scot and William Seman are listed in that entry and they also appear in the extent (fol. 159v). Scot was from Wherstead (Werestede), a little to the east of Gusford.

[132] See the TNA website where the manor is named Goddlesford: https://discovery.nationalar-chives.gov.uk/details/c/F250441 [accessed 22 Oct. 2024]. This extent therefore provides some very welcome new information about the manor in this period before the Black Death.

Table 22. The values and acreages of the holdings within the manor of Gusford.

	Item	Size (acres, rods, perches)	Value (£ s d)	Note
The demesne	The court close	3.5a 1r 24p	*2s*	
	The fruits of the trees		*18d*	
	Arable land	65a 1r 3p	*17s 5¾d*	
	Meadowland	10a 1r 25p	*16s 3½d*	
	Woodland	14.5a	*6s*	
Demesne sub-total		*94a 12p*	*43s 3¼d*	
	The watermill		*40s*	
	The perquisites of the manorial and leet courts		*20s*	
Rents				
	Of the freemen	81a 1r	*34s*	
	From the occupants of bonded tenements	45a	*17s 4d*	
	From the services and works of bonded tenements		*29s 10⅜d*	
Rents and services sub-total			*£4 1s 2½d*	
Grand total		220a 1r 12p	*£9 4s 5½d*	Value rounded down fractionally to a halfpenny

The demesne comprised a little under a half of the total acreage, and the value was also under half of the combined demesne and tenanted land. The value of demesne only just exceeded that of the watermill, which, at 40s, was clearly an important element of the abbey's income. Within the section listing the free tenants, there are twenty-two names, of whom two hold cottages. Of the bonded tenancies, five are held by serfs (*nativi*), while five are held by tenants described as free in body (*liber corpore*). This low proportion of serf tenants is similar to the level seen at Sheddon and much lower than some of Canonsleigh's western manors such as Hockford or Northleigh.

The above table shows that two courts were in operation within this manor. The manorial court (*curia manerii*, in later times known as the court baron) was a

Fig. 8. BL Add. MS 10293, fol. 261r. A novice nun has her tresses removed.

common feature of English manorial administration and met frequently, typically once every three weeks. The leet court met only once or twice a year and was more properly called the view of frankpledge (*visus francplegii*).[133] The entry for the free tenant Andrew Arunde on fol. 159v suggests that the date for the annual court leet came just after Michaelmas (29 September).

One commercial activity providing moderate income at Gusford was the management and sale of coppice wood. The extent describes 14½ acres of such wood (*silva cedua*) that was never allowed to grow beyond five years before being cut down. In normal years, the wood so harvested had a value of 30s and a portion was put aside for sale with a value of 5s (fol. 159r).

Among the free tenants is listed the prior of Ipswich (*Prior Sancti Petri de Zypeswych*). The Priory of Saints Peter and Paul had been founded as a house for Augustinian canons in around 1189.[134] The prior in 1323 was Henry of Kersey, who had been elected in 1311.[135] He had two holdings, of which the second was just half

---

[133] For a brief introduction to the system of manorial courts see Bailey, *The English Manor*, pp. 167–84. Bailey acknowledges his debt to the 'monumental' study of *Medieval Society and the Manor Court*, ed. by Zvi Razi and Richard Michael Smith (Clarendon Press, 1996), doi:10.1093/acprof:oso/9780198201908.001.0001.

[134] Knowles, *Medieval Religious Houses, England and Wales*, p. 141.

[135] David M. Smith and Vera C. M. London, *The Heads of Religious Houses: England and Wales II, 1216–1377*, The Heads of Religious Houses Series, 1st edn (Cambridge University Press, 2001), p. 396, doi:10.1017/CBO9780511495632.

an acre, for which he owed 1*d* in rent. The first of his holdings was the land of Douninggeslonde, which he held until the heir of that estate, Alice, came of age. The prior owed rent of 3*s* for that property (fol. 160r).

A particular concern for the surveyor was the moveable feast of Easter. On fol. 162r, he wrote a detailed memorandum pointing out that there could be duplication of services for tenants such as Geoffrey and Hamond Douelers. They were bound by obligations to perform works from Michaelmas until Easter within a three-year cycle. As that period could vary by over a month, then it was possible for the length of the cycle to fall below thirty-six months. This could lead to some duplication in the third year. There might also be an impact on other summer and autumn works. The surveyor may have been especially conscious of the effect of a changeable Easter date from recent years. In 1315, Easter had been early (23 March), while in 1318 it had been late (23 April). Shortly afterwards, there had been another expression of that changeability – Easter fell on 19 April in 1321 but on 27 March in 1323.[136]

A Query Concerning Mills

Two entries in the extents concern the transportation of millstones – see fol. 141r for the manor of Netherton and fol. 143v for the manor of Rockbeare. Both entries are puzzling. That for Netherton talks of the millstone being carried to the third purchaser (*tertio emptori*), while that for Rockbeare talks of carriage to the second purchaser (*secondo emptori*). One possible interpretation is that by purchaser is meant the farmer or leasor of the mill. The period of that rental would be determined by the length of their lease. For a mill, that would typically have been for something like seven years.[137] Thus to talk about an event fourteen or more years in the future would seem odd. Another possible interpretation is that the current farmer is the second or third one in that manor, but that the surveyor is coy about naming them explicitly. However, the extents are full of the names of tenants, benefactors and others, so it would again seem odd if the leasors of the mills were not named. A third possibility is that the purchasers were outsiders who were buying used millstones second- or third-hand from the abbey. New millstones were expensive to purchase and transport, and there was certainly a trade in millstones that could be refurbished and brought back into use.[138]

Editorial Notes

Like all survey documents of the late medieval period, the Canonsleigh extents include much content that is formulaic. For that reason, a good proportion of the entries are given here in slightly summarised form rather than being written out in full. The complete content for one Devon manor, that of Netherton in the parish of Farway, is provided as Appendix 1. The full English translation is there, together with a copy of the Latin text. In the manuscript, the scribe used common abbreviations to

---

[136] All dates taken from C. R. Cheney and Michael Jones, *A Handbook of Dates for Students of British History*, Royal Historical Society Guides and Handbooks; No. 4, new edn/revised by Michael Jones (Cambridge University Press, 2000), p. 229.
[137] John Langdon, *Mills in the Medieval Economy: England, 1300–1540*, Oxford Scholarship Online, 1st edn (Oxford University Press, 2004), p. 189, doi:10.1093/oso/9780199265589.001.0001.
[138] Richard Holt, *The Mills of Medieval England* (Basil Blackwell, 1988), p. 177.

save time and ink – in the Appendix, those abbreviations have all been expanded to give the complete Latin text.

All dates in this document are given in modern format. Until the introduction of the Gregorian calendar into England in 1752, the new year officially began on 25 March. Thus the year 1323 had begun on 25 March (Lady Day, the feast of the Annunciation) and ran until the following 24 March. In this publication, 1 January is treated as the start of each year. Thus what the medieval writer would have written as 10 January 1322 would here be written as 10 January 1323.

Within this Introduction, any text in Latin is given in italics.

In the extents, all first names are written using their modern English equivalent (thus *Johannes* as John, *Henricus* as Henry, *Alicia* as Alice etc.).[139] All surnames, even where there may be an obvious modern equivalent, are left as written by the medieval surveyor (thus *Baldewine*, not Baldwin).

The sizes of land holdings are commonly given as acres, rods and perches. There are 4 rods to an acre and 40 perches to a rod. Rods and perches may also be used as linear measures but here should be treated as measurements of area, thus square rods and square perches.

Monetary values are normally given as pounds (£ or *libre*),[140] shillings (*s* or *solidi*) and pence (*d* or *denarii*). There were 12 pence to a shilling and 20 shillings to a pound. Another commonly used value was the mark, which had a value of two-thirds of a pound, thus 13 shillings and 4 pence; a half mark was valued at 6 shillings and 8 pence and a quarter mark at 3 shillings and 4 pence.

---

[139] A list of Latin first names can be found in C. T. Martin, *The Record Interpreter: A Collection of Abbreviations, Latin Words and Names Used in English Historical Manuscripts and Records* (Reeves & Turner, 1892), pp. 334–9. This book is available as a free download.

[140] In classical Latin the nominative plural of the feminine noun *libra* would be *librae*; here the medieval pluralization method is used, hence *libre*.

THE EXTENTS SECTION A

THE WEST COUNTRY MANORS

MANOR OF LEIGH

[*Legh*]

Extent of the manor of Leigh of the Canonesses made there by the men of that same manor, namely William Bysouthedone, Walter Vorst, Luke de Hountelonde, William de Westecote, John Fendur, Adam Baldewine, Thomas atte Shuete, John Portere, William Aluard, George Smith [*Fabrum*] and Roger Coleman, jurors one and all by the homage of the said manor. This extent was made on Sunday on the day after [the feast of] Saint Barnabas the Apostle in the year of our Lord 1323 and the third year of lady Margaret [Aunger] as abbess.[1]

[*Demesne*]

[*Arable land*]

In the field division [*forlang*] next to the grange of the court towards the west in Ouereforland 18½ acres; in Nythereforlang 19 acres 1 rod; in Pylelonde 18½ acres; in Oldemarnelonde 19 acres 1 rod; in Haybeare 12½ acres; in Nyenakerlond 9 acres; in Pugeham towards the land of Pouke de Geffreyshulle 12 acres; in Knollelond 22½ acres; in Seleham 28½ acres; in Langemede 2½ acres 1 rod; in Les Byrches 12 acres; in la Legh 8½ acres; in a piece of cultivated land [*una cultura*] above la Knolle 4½ acres; in another such piece next to the fowling-glade [*volatile*] of the woodcocks 3½ acres; in Wolle Legh 3½ acres; in the whole of Byestebrok 50½ acres.

The sum of acres of the aforementioned arable land 245 acres 1 rod. The value per acre for the extent, more or less, 4d.
Thus in total £4 21d.

[*Meadows*]

In Nythereforlang next to the aforesaid grange within the ditch [*fossatum*] 12 acres; outside the ditch 7 acres; in EsteWille 7 acres; in Pylelondesfote 2½ acres; in Crossemede beneath Eldemarnelond with Wylbelesheye 4½ acres; in Nycholeshamme 6½ acres; in Pugeham 2 acres 1 rod; in Poulemede 6½ acres 1 rod; in Knollelonde 2½ acres; in Louenalre 2 acres; in Selehammede 3 acres 1 rod; in Holemede 1 acre; in Suthpolemede 7½ acres; in Middelpolemede 2½ acres 1 rod; in Northpolemede 5 acres 1 rod.

The sum of the acres of meadow 72 acres 1 rod.
The acre by the extent above is worth 12d. Thus in total 72s.

---

[1] Sunday, 12 June 1323.

[*Moor*]

In Nycholeshamme and Wyblesheye 5½ acres; in Pugeham 2½ acres; in Redyngalres next to Roweknolle 8 acres; in Polealres 4 acres; in the park next to Coluereheye 12 acres; in Estebroke 4½ acres; in Geffreyesalres 2½ acres; in la Botme 2 acres.

The sum of the acres of moor 41 acres.
The value per acre in the extent above 5d. Thus in total 17s 1d.

[*Woodland*]

In Roweknolle 6½ acres; in Oxeslade 10 acres.

The sum of acres of woodland 16½ acres.
The value per acre in the extent above 5d. Thus in total 6s 10½d.

[*Waste land*]

In Eldemarlelond 13 acres; in Pugeham next to Nyenacres 12 acres; beneath Geffreyeshull 9 acres; in Les Byrches 20 acres; in the land of Byestebroke 6 acres.

The sum of acres of waste land 60 acres.
The value per acre in the extent above 2d. Thus in total 10s.
The total value of the aforesaid land with meadow, moor and wood in the extent above
£9 7s 11½d.

[*Gardens, dove-cot, mill*]

There are 4 gardens adjoining the court of the abbey of Leigh valued at 4*s*.
A dove-cot valued at 2*s*.
A mill at Pugeham valued at 26*s* 8*d*.

The sum of the value of those 32s 8d.

[*The church of Burlescombe [Burwoldescumbe]*]

The church of Burlescombe is appropriated to the said abbey and is taxed at the true value of 60*s*.

The total is 60s.

The total value of the entire aforesaid demesne with the church of Burlescombe £14
7½d.

[*Thorne St Margaret, Somerset [Thorne, Somersete]*]

[*Arable land*]

In Henriescrofte 15 acres; in Swetewodecrofte 6 acres; in Muntelonde next to the marl pit 8 acres; next to Blakepole 9 acres; beneath Blakepole 6½ acres; beneath the Grange of Somerset [*subtus Grangiam de Somersete*] 12½ acres 1 rod; in the southern part of the same grange 13 acres worth 3*d* per acre.

The sum of the acres of arable land 70 acres 1 rod and the value per acre is as above. Thus in total the value is 17s 6¾d.

[*Meadows*]

In Shyreburneforde 3½ acres; in Wetemede 1 acre. Value per acre 12*d*.

The sum of the acres of meadow 4½ acres, value per acre as above. Thus in total the value is 4s 6d.

[*Waste land*]

In Estedoune 27½ acres 1 rod; in Gapereslade 31 acres; beneath Maysenewylle 28 acres; in Suthmaydene Wibbedoune 72 acres; in Northdoune 51 acres; next to la Holoke 3 acres.

The sum of the acres is 212½ acres 1 rod.
Value per acre for the above extent 1d. Thus in total the sum of the value is 17s 8¾d.

[*Woods*]

In Shortewode 3 acres farmed out [*arentantur*] to Roger de Burdesleghe below within the 5 acres he holds, and therefore they do not fall [*non cadunt hic*] within the extent here.

The sum of the value of the demesne of Leigh with the church of Burlescombe and with Thorne in Somerset in the aforesaid extent £16 5d.

[*The fixed rents of the lords who hold nothing from the said abbey but rather from their gift through their charters*][2]

From John de Clavile, the tithe of his rent in Burlescombe [*Burwoldescumbe*]; 8*s* at the four principal terms of the year, from his chamber.

From the same John at the same terms; 3*s* that were restored to Roger de Clavile in front of the itinerant justices of the lord king in Burlescombe, as is clear from the fine levied in the presence of the said itinerant justice between the prior of Leigh and the

---

[2]   These lords had granted such rents to the priory or abbey in addition to any grants of land etc. Of the seven items listed all but the first have a corresponding entry in the *Cartulary*. In order, for item two onwards, these are entry numbers 26, 28, 30, 58, 55 and 33.

said Roger de Clavile which outcome can be learned in the charters of the lords of Clavile at number XV.

From the same John at the same terms by a certain Thomas de Deaudone; 12*d* as is shown in the charter of the said Roger de Clavile at number XVII.

From the same John the tithe of his rent at Morden [*Mordone*] at the same terms; 8*s* as is shown in the charter of Walter de Clavile, the founder of the monastery of Leigh, at number XVI.

From John de Aysforde; 12*d* owing for the soul of John, son of William de Aysforde for his anniversary held on the third day next after the feast of Saint Gregory the Pope as is shown in the charter of William de Aysforde at number V,[3] and by the confirmation of Arthur de Aysforde at number VII.

From the said John de Aysforde; 4*s* as is shown in his charter at number IV.

From Hugh de Raleghe from the tithe of his rent in Wydecumbe; 3*s* 4*d* that were granted to the said monastery by Walter de Clavile payable annually on the feast of Saint Michael as is shown by the charter of the same Hugh at the end of the charters of Clavile at number XVII.

Total 31s.

[*Free tenants*]

The abbot of Dunkeswell [*Doneskes Wylle*] holds a certain tenement in Schallecumbe; 5*s* annually at the feast of Saint Michael. It is not known if he owes any other service for the same and thus it should be investigated.

The heirs of lord Thomas de Cirencester [*Cyrcestre*], knight, holds in Childelomene at la Beare a ferling of land by charter; 2*s* 8*d* annually at the four principal terms.[4] It is not known if he owes any other service for the same and thus it should be investigated.

Roger Bysouthezo [*Bysoutheye, Bysoulheye*] holds 1 ferling of land at Cadewylle by charter;[5] 5*s* at the aforesaid terms. It is not known if he owes any other service for the same and thus it should be investigated.

The same Roger holds one other ferling of land at will; 5*s* at the said terms for all service except for suit at the court of the ladies of Leigh at Leigh.

Robert le Porter holds the land of Pynstonslade for his lifetime and that of his son, Richard; 12*s* 6*d* at the aforesaid terms for all service except suit of court as above.

John the Miller [*Molendinarius*] holds the mill at Pugeham and 3 acres of land for his

---

3   The feast of Gregory the Great falls on 3 September.
4   Thomas of Cirencester was sheriff of Devon 1231 – *Cartulary* item 20.
5   Roger was proctor of the canonesses – *Cartulary* items 277 and 278.

lifetime by charter; 2*s* at the said terms for all service except suit of court and royal service.

Richard Bastard holds a certain tenement in Cadewylle; 2*s* at the said terms, but it is not known how he holds it nor for how long and therefore it should be investigated.

Robert Coleman holds 2 ferlings of land in Passemeresheyes; 10*s* at the aforesaid terms. It is not known if he owes any service and therefore it should be investigated.

John the Baker [*Pistor*] holds at will a third part of 1 ferling of land at Holebroke; 2*s* 6*d* at the said terms for all service except suit of court and heriot of his best beast due upon his death or upon surrender.

William Palmere holds at will another third part of the same ferling; 21*d* at the said terms for all service except suit of court and heriot as above.

Roger atte More holds at will the other third part of the same ferling; 21*d* at the said terms for all service except suit of court and heriot as above.

John the Baker holds the mill at Knaphille [*Knappemulle*]; 12*s* at the said terms for all service except suit of court. He will uphold all the customs of that same mill except for the timber and the millstones that the ladies of Leigh will provide together with the carriage of them to the said mill.

John Attebronnehulle holds by charter for his lifetime and for that of his wife Margery 1 ferling of land in Estebroke; 6*s* 6*d* at the said terms for all service except suit of court and royal service.

Roger de Berdesleghe holds at will 5 acres of land in Berdesleghe at Sandgete below Shortewode; 3*s* 4*d* at the said terms for all service except suit of court and heriot as above.

Matilda de Harpeford holds by charter 2 ferlings of land in Byrdesleghe; 4*s* at the said terms. It is not known if she owes any other service and therefore it should be investigated.

Ralph de Pouleshele holds by charter 3 acres of land in Thorne St Margaret next to Shortewode; 1 rose [*rosam*].[6] It is not known if he owes any other service and therefore it should be investigated.

Simon Bloyou holds by charter 3 acres of land in Berdesleghe next to la Pytte; ½*d* at the feast of Saint Michael. It is not known if he owes any other service and therefore it should be investigated.

---

[6] The rose was a form of quit-rent and was not uncommon in the later medieval period. The city of York provides many examples of this (see Sarah Ruth Rees Jones, 'Property, Tenure and Rents: Some Aspects of the Topography and Economy of Medieval York, Vol. 2' (unpublished doctoral thesis, University of York, 1987), viewable at https://etheses.whiterose.ac.uk/id/eprint/4273/2/DX081136_2.pdf [accessed 5 Feb. 2025]).

Richard de la Hale holds by charter half a virgate of land in Thorne St Margaret; a pair of white spurs or 2d on the feast of Saint Michael; and also he provided fealty to the lady abbess of Leigh at Leigh on the Tuesday immediately before the feast of Saint George the Martyr in the 14th year of the reign of King Edward son of King Edward.[7] It is not known if he must do anything more and therefore it should be investigated.

Richard Attehulle holds by charter 3 acres of land in Thorne at Chaldewylle; ½d at the feast of St Michael. It is not known if he must do anything more and therefore it should be investigated.

The same Richard de la Hale holds by charter in Brompton Ralph [*Brumpton Radulphi*] 1 ferling of land; 6d on the feast of Saint Michael.[8] It is not known if he must do anything more and therefore it should be investigated. He provided fealty to the said lady abbess as described previously on the Tuesday in the year as above.

Philip Burdesleghe holds by charter half a virgate of land there by hereditary right; 2s at the feast of Saint Michael. His heirs will provide feudal relief on the death of their father.[9]

The heirs of Jordan Byturt of Milverton hold 2 acres in Milverton; 6s at the feast of Saint Michael and the feast of Saint John the Baptist in equal portions for those 2 acres in Milverton that the Jordan himself held from Roger Kyng, paying to him the aforesaid rent; that same Roger Kyng bestowed the said rent for the said Jordan to pay to the monastery of Leigh for ever in pure and perpetual alms as shown in the charter of that Roger Kyng at number XXXI.

The heirs of Richard le Hopere hold ½ acre of land in Milverton; 3s at the said terms of Saint John and Saint Michael in equal portions that this Richard held from that Roger le Kyng, paying himself the aforementioned rent, and the same Roger le Kyng assigned that rent for Richard to pay in pure and perpetual alms for ever to the monastery of Leigh as shown in the charter of the aforesaid Roger next above number XXXI.

The heirs of John de Arundel and of Nicholas son of Martin from the land of de la Bere for one perpetual chaplain to celebrate divine service for the soul of the said John and his ancestors; 60s at Easter or on the octave of Easter as is shown in his charter at number XIIII.

The heirs of William de Bosco for the land of Swetatone; 2s that Amice, at one time wife of William de Bosco senior, gave to the said monastery in pure and perpetual alms as is shown in the charter of the same Amice at number II.
The heirs of William son of William de Bosco of 3½ acres of assart in Contescumbe;

---

[7] Wednesday, 22 April 1321.
[8] A note was added in the right margin saying *que vocatur heaundon* (that is called Heaundon).
[9] There is a manicule in the left margin pointing at this entry.

6*d* that the said William gave to the monastery as is shown in the charter of that same William at number III.

The heirs of William de Bosco for the rent that Stephen de Wadetone was accustomed to bear; 6*d* as is shown in the charter of the said William at number V.

Richard de Choseldene for the land of Gorewylle; 6*s* at the said terms.

Robert Attemere for the land of Gemyaneswalles in the parish of Rose Ash [*Esse Radulphi*]; 2*s* on the feast of Pentecost with deliverance by the sacrist for the reeve.

The heirs of Nicholas son of Walter for 1 ferling of land that Robert, lord of Morleghe, gave; 2*s* due on the day of Saint Michael.[10]

The mill at Wydecumbe and 6 acres of land there; 12*s* per annum in the hand of lord Hugh de Courtenay [*Curteney*].[11]

A certain tenement in Hempston [*Hemmestone*] with 6 acres of land that John Arundel gave to the monastery with the advowson of the same church; 2*s* as is shown in the first charter for Hempston.

The heirs of Baldwin for Thomas Berdeslegh; 2*s* at the feast of Saint Michael as is shown in the charter VI of Baldwin de Thorne.

A half virgate of land that Geoffrey son of Alured held in Berdesleghe; 4*s* as is shown in the charter IX of Baldwin of Thorne.

John de Holeweye holds 1 tenement in Blackborough [*Blakeburghe*]; 3*s* 4*d* at the four aforesaid terms, which rent he ceased to pay from the time of the acquisition of the same tenement from William Holeweye, his father.

The heirs of William Lamprey for a certain piece of land at Byestebroke that Emery [surname left blank] once held through the hand of those who held that same land; 12*d* at the four aforesaid terms.

The heirs of Simon of Greenham [*Gryndham*] for the land of de la Torre through the hand of those who held that land; 12*s* and sufficient stone from that land for the roofing of his church and his houses at Leigh.

The heirs of Robert de Morleghe for 1 ferling of land in Morleghe; 12*d* at the nativity of the Lord and at the feast of Saint John the Baptist as is shown in the charter of the same Robert.

---

[10]   There is a manicule in the margin pointing up to this entry. This entry and those of all the remaining free tenants are prefaced by the word *de*. It is not clear why the scribe chose to do so, unless it was to show that all those entries should be given special attention.

[11]   This is probably Hugh de Courtenay (1275–1340) who was also a benefactor of Torre Abbey; see for example John Christopher Jenkins, 'Torre Abbey: Locality, Community and Society in Medieval Devon' (unpublished doctoral thesis, University of Oxford, 2010), p. 109.

The heirs of William of Crues for his tenement in Nytherexe; 1 pound of wax at the feast of Saint Michael or in the octave of the same feast.

The total rent of the free tenants £9 6s 5d and 1 pound of wax, whence from the farm of the mill 12s.[12]

[*Tenants at will in bondage*]

William Bysouthedone holds at Bysouthedon 1 virgate of land and he is free in body; 5*s* in equal portions at the four principal terms of the year.

> He will plough for 1 day in the winter with his tithing-men and he will have lunch once in the day with his tithing-men. If he does not plough he will give 4*d* for his aforesaid plough-service.

> He will harrow once in the winter with his own harrow and animal and he will have food once in the day, and if he does not do harrow-service he will give ½*d* for it.

> He will plough twice in Lent and he will have food once in the day. If he does not plough then he will give 5*d* for each day of plough-service.

> Similarly he will harrow twice at that season and he will have his meal once in the day. If he does not harrow he will give ½*d* for each day of harrowing-service.

> He will hoe for 1 half day for which he will have nothing. If he does not hoe then he will give ½*d* for that work.

> He will mow for 1 day and he will have a meal twice in the day. That work is worth 1*d*.

> He will reap for 3 days in the autumn and he will have food twice in the day when he reaps. The work of one day is worth 1*d*.

> He himself with Thomas Dun his neighbour will, with his wagon and oxen, carry hay to the mill in Barton for one day. They will have food twice in the day and their work is worth 6*d*.

> And they will carry the beans in the same way for 1 day and the work is worth 6*d*.

> And they will do carriage-service twice to Exeter or to Topsham [*Tuppesham*] or to another place where on the second day it is possible to return home, seeking salt or corn, and then he will take some salt or 4 bushels of toll-corn [*duro blado*] or 6 bushels of large oats or a quarter of small oats, and when he returns home with his wagon as aforesaid, then he will have 5 chopps and a quarter,[13] and one carriage-service is worth 2*d*.

> He will clean the mill-leat for half a day with others of his neighbours and for that he will have nothing. The work is worth ½*d*.

> And so the services of this aforesaid William are worth 2*s* 4½*d*.

> He will give 18*d* as tallage on the feast of Saint Michael.[14]

---

[12] Some further text was added in a less formal hand to say 'they were produced in services and not in rent' (*qui ciuerunt in serviciis et non in redditu*).

[13] The chopp (*choppa*) appears to be some form of food, but its exact meaning is not known.

[14] For William Bysouthedone and the other bonded tenants, the scribe notes in the margin that

He will be reeve if he is elected and then he will be quit of his rent and of his works.

He will give his best beast for heriot and his second best beast as a mortuary payment when he dies.

He cannot have his son educated nor see his daughter married, nor can he sell his male colt or his foal or his ox or his calf without the permission of his ladies.

Thomas Dun, villein of the ladies, holds 1 ferling of land at Suthedon; 3s at the said terms.

He, with Alice atte Slade his neighbour, will plough once in winter and twice in Lent and he will have food as above, and his services for that are worth 7d.

He will harrow for 1 day and for a half day with food as above and the work is worth ¾d.

He will mow for 1 day with food as above and the work is worth 1d.

He will reap for 3 days with food as above and the work is worth 3d.

He will carry the hay and beans of the ladies to their Barton for 2 days with his oxen in association with the above-mentioned William Bysouthedon with food, and that service for himself is worth 6d.

He will do carrying-service twice just as the aforesaid William and the service is worth 4d.

He will clean the mill-leat as above and the work is worth ½d.

He will give a heriot and mortuary payment as above.

He will be the reeve if he is elected to such and then he will be quit of his services.

He cannot have his son educated nor see his daughter married, nor can he sell his colt or his ox without the permission of the ladies.

His services are worth 22¾d.

He will give 6d as tallage.

Alice atte Slade, free in body, holds at atte Slade ½ ferling of land; 4s at the said terms.

She will plough with Thomas Dun as stated before, just as [described] in the services of the same Thomas and the service is worth 7d.

She will reap for 3 days with food as above and the service is worth 3d.

She will clean the mill-leat for a half day and the work is worth ½d.

No other service is required for that same tenement, but if a man held the same tenement he would be reeve if he were elected. Then he would be quit of the aforesaid rent and services.

The aforesaid services are worth 10½d.

She will give nothing as tallage.

---

tallage (*auxilium*) is owing and the amount.

Robert de Pugeham, free in body, holds ½ acre of land in Pugeham; 8s 4d at the said terms.

> He will reap for 3 days as above and the work is worth 3d.
>
> If he is elected he will be reeve and he will be quit of 5s of his rent and of his services.
>
> His services are worth 3d.
>
> He will give nothing as tallage.

Luke de Huntelond, free in body, holds ½ ferling of land in Huntelond; 3s at the said terms.

> He will plough once in winter and once during Lent with food and the service is worth 9d.
>
> He will hoe for half a day and the service is worth ½d.
>
> He will mow for 1 day with food and the work is worth 1d.
>
> He will do hay-making for half a day and the work is worth ½d.
>
> He will mow 4½ acres of meadow as is the custom for those 9d owing from his rent on the feast of Saint John the Baptist. For that he will have 2 chopps and 1 pot of the usual ale for whatever acre he will mow. The service is worth 3½d.
>
> He will reap for 3 days with food and the work is worth 3d.
>
> He will help with the making of the hay-cocks in the Barton for 1 day and for another day at the making of the bean stack with food and the work is worth 2d.
>
> He will clean the mill-leat and the work is worth ½d.
>
> He will be the reeve if elected and then he will be quit as above.
>
> He will do 2 carrying-services as above. The service is worth 4d.
>
> His services besides the tallage are worth 2s.
>
> He will give 6d as tallage.

Richard de Goldemore, free in body, holds two tenements in Goldemore; 6s at the said terms.

> He will plough twice in winter and twice during Lent and the service is worth 18d.
>
> He will hoe for half a day with 2 men and the work is worth ½d.
>
> He will mow for 1 day with 2 men with food and the work is worth 2d.
>
> He will help with the hay-making for half a day with 2 men and the work is worth 1d.
>
> He will do 2 carrying-services with 2 men and 2 beasts and the service is worth 8d.
>
> He will help to make the hay-cocks in the Barton for 1 day with 2 men and the bean stack with 2 men for 1 day with food and the work is worth 4d.
>
> He will reap for 2 days with 2 men with food and the service is worth 6d.
>
> He will clean the mill-leat with 2 men and the work is worth 1d.

He will mow 9 acres of meadow as is the custom for 18*d* from his rent for his two tenements from the term of Saint John the Baptist, receiving for that work the same as the aforesaid Luke. The service is worth 7*d*.

His works except for his tallage are worth 4*s*.

He will give 2*s* as tallage for his 2 tenements.

John de Westecote, free in body, holds ½ ferling in Westecote; 4*s* at the said terms.

He will plough for 1 day in winter and for another day during Lent. The service is worth 9*d*.

He will hoe for half a day and the work is worth ½*d*.

He will mow for 1 day and the work is worth 1*d*.

He will do hay-making for half a day and the work is worth ½*d*.

He will reap for 3 days and the work is worth 3*d*.

He will do 2 carrying-services and the service is worth 4*d*.

He will help to make the hay-cocks for 1 day and the bean stack for another day and the work is worth 2*d*.

He will clean the mill-leat for half a day and the work is worth ½*d*.

He will mow 4½ acres of meadow as is the custom for 9*d* from his rent from the term of Saint John the Baptist and for that he will receive the same as the aforesaid Luke. The service is worth 3½*d*.

His works besides tallage are worth 2*s*.

He will give tallage of 6*d*.

Walter Coviyn Byestebrok, free in body, holds ½ ferling of land at Byestebrok; 4*s* at the said terms.

He will plough a half day of plough-service for the winter-sown crop and for 1 day in Lent and the service is worth 7*d*.

He will hoe for half a day and the work is worth ½*d*.

He will mow for 1 day and the work is worth 1*d*.

He will do hay-making for half a day and work is worth ½*d*.

He will help with the making of the hay-cocks and the bean stack and the work is worth 2*d*.

He will reap for 3 days and the work is worth 3*d*.

He will clean the mill-leat and the work is worth ½*d*.

He will perform 2 carrying-services and the service is worth 4*d*.

He will mow 4½ acres as is the custom for 9*d* from his rent from the term of Saint John the Baptist and for that will receive the same as the aforesaid Luke and the service is worth 3½*d*.

His works excepting tallage are worth 22*d*.

He will give tallage of 6*d*.

He will be reeve if elected to this.

William de Westcote, free in body, holds a close of land in Westecote; 2*s* at the said terms.

> He, with his neighbour, Richard de Westecote, will plough once in winter and once in Lent and the services of the two of them are worth 9*d*.
>
> They will hoe for half a day and their work is worth ½*d*.
>
> They will reap for 3 days with 1 man and the work is worth 1*d*.
>
> They will help with making the hay-cocks and the bean stack for 2 days with 1 man and the work is worth 2*d*.
>
> They will perform 2 carrying-services and their work is worth 4*d*.
>
> They will clean the mill-leat with 1 man for half a day and their work is worth ½*d*.
>
> They must mow as is the custom 3 acres of meadow jointly for 6*d* from their rent on the feast of Saint John the Baptist and for that work they will have 6 chopps and 3 pots of familiar ale, one having 3 chopps and 3 quarts of ale and the other just as much.
>
> The value of their services in this is 2½*d*.
>
> The works of them jointly are worth 22½*d*.
>
> He will give 3*d* as tallage.

Richard de Westecote, free in body, holds 1 close in Westecote; 12*d* at the said terms.

> He will do services with William de Westecote his neighbour named above, that are described and valued in the service of the same William. The value of their services is stated above.
>
> They will not be reeves.
>
> He will give 3*d* as tallage.

Walter Vorst, free in body, holds a dwelling-house [*mansum*] and 5 acres of land; 3*s* 2*d* at the said terms.

> He will hoe for half a day and the work is worth ½*d*.
>
> He will mow for 1 day with food and the work is worth 1*d*.
>
> He will do hay-making for half a day and the work is worth ½*d*.
>
> He will reap for 3 days as above and the work is worth 3*d*.
>
> He will help with making the hay-cocks and the bean stack for another day and the work is worth 2*d*.
>
> He will clean the mill-leat for half a day and the work is worth ½*d*.
>
> He will mow 4½ acres of meadow as is the custom for 9*d* from his rent from the term of Saint John the Baptist and for that he will receive the same as the aforesaid Luke and the service is worth 3½*d*.
>
> He will do trench-work for 1 day in the winter and for that he will have food once and the work is worth ½*d*.
>
> His aforesaid works are worth 11½*d*.
>
> He will give 6*d* as tallage.
>
> He will be reeve.

William Bearde, free in body, holds a dwelling-house and 3 acres of land in Estobrok; 2s at the said terms.

He will hoe for a half day and the work is worth ½d.

He will help with the hay-making for half a day and the work is worth ½d.

He will reap for 3 days with food as above, and beyond this he will have 2 chopps for supper on every night he reaps. The work is worth 3d.

He will help with making the hay-cocks and the bean stack for another day with food and in the evening [in sero] 2 chopps. The work is worth 2d.

He will clean the mill-leat and the work is worth ½d.

He will do trench-work for 1 day and the work is worth ½d.

Thus his works are worth 7d.

He will give nothing as tallage.

John the Smith [Faber], free in body, holds a dwelling-house in Burwoldescumbe atte Wylle and 5 acres of land; 4s 6d, namely at Christmas 7½d, at Easter 7½d, at the feast of Saint John the Baptist 7½d, and at the feast of Saint Michael 2s 7½d.

He will hoe for a half day and the work is worth ½d.

He will mow for 1 day with food and in the evening he will have 3 chopps and the work is worth 1d.

He will do hay-making for half a day and the work is worth ½d.

He will reap for 3 days with food twice in the day and in the evening 2 chopps and the work is worth 3d.

He will help with the making of the hay-cocks and the bean stack with food as above and in the evening 2 chopps. The work is worth 2d.

The aforesaid works are worth 7d.

He will give 6d as tallage.

William Burdoun, villein, holds a dwelling-house and 3 acres of land in Westecote; 3s at the said terms.

He will hoe for half a day and the work is worth ½d.

He will mow for 1 day with food as above and in the evening he will have 2 chopps. The service is worth 1d.

He will help with the hay-making for half a day and the work is worth ½d.

He will reap for 3 days with food as above and in the evening he will have 2 chopps. The work is worth 3d.

He will help with making the hay-cocks and the bean stack with food as above and in the evening he will have 2 chopps. The work is worth 2d.

He will clean the mill-leat and the work is worth ½d.

He will do trench-work as above and the work is worth ½d.

His works are worth 8d.

He will give nothing as tallage.

Hugh le Combere, free in body, holds a dwelling-house with curtilage in Westecote; 18*d* at the said terms for all service. He will give nothing as tallage.

Robert Hayrun, villein, holds a dwelling-house and 2 acres of land in Pugeham; 3*s* 4*d* at the said terms.

> He will reap for 3 days with food as above and in the evening when he reaps he will have 2 chopps. The service is worth 3*d*.
>
> His services are worth 3*d*.
>
> He will give nothing as tallage.

William Louel, villein, holds a dwelling-house and 5 acres of land in Westlegh; 3*s* at the said terms.

> He will hoe for a half day and the work is worth ½*d*.
>
> He will mow for 1 day with food as above and the work is worth 1*d*.
>
> He will do hay-making for half a day and the work is worth ½*d*.
>
> He will reap for 3 days with food as above and the work is worth 3*d*.
>
> He will help with the making of the hay-cocks and the bean stack for 2 days with food as above and the work is worth 2*d*.
>
> He will cleanse the mill-leat and the work is worth ½*d*.
>
> He will mow 4½ acres of meadow as is the custom for 9*d* from his rent from the term of Saint John the Baptist and he will receive the same as Luke above for that and the work is worth 3½*d*.
>
> He will do trench-work for 1 day as above and the work is worth ½*d*.
>
> His works are worth 11½*d*.
>
> He will give 6*d* as tallage.

Richard Wytenon, villein, holds 1 dwelling-house and 5 acres of land in Westlegh; 3*s* 6*d* at the said terms.

> He will do all the same services as William Louel.
>
> His works are worth 11½*d*.
>
> He will give 6*d* as tallage.

Agnes Coleman holds 1 dwelling-house and 5 acres of land; 3*s* at the said terms.

> She will do all the same services as William Louel.
>
> Her works are worth 11½*d*.
>
> She will give 6*d* as tallage.

John Fendur, villein, holds 1 dwelling-house and 5 acres of land in Westlegh; 3*s* 4*d* at the said terms.

> He will do all the same services as William Louel.
>
> His works are worth 11½*d*.
>
> He will give 6*d* as tallage.

William atte Knolle, free in body, holds a cottage with curtilage in Westlegh; 2*s* at the said terms for all service.

Alice Hertes, villein, holds a cottage with curtilage in Westlegh; 16*d* for all service.

Simon Breye,[15] free in body, holds a cottage with curtilage in Westlegh; 18*d* at the said terms for all service.

Robert Hareuest, free in body, holds a cottage with curtilage in Westlegh; 18*d* at the said terms for all service.

Christine Daeymele, free in body, holds a cottage with curtilage in Burlescombe [*Burwoldescumbe*]; 2*s* 4*d* at the said terms.

> She will reap for 2 days with food as above and in the evening she will have 2 chopps when she reaps. The work is worth 2*d*.
>
> Her work is worth 2*d*.

Adam Baldewine of Thorne Margaret, villein, holds 1 ferling of land in Thorne; 5*s* 6*d* at the said terms.

> He will plough for 1 day in winter and another day in Lent with another neighbour of his and he will have food as above. The service is worth 9*d*.
>
> He will do hay-making for half a day and the work is worth ½*d*.
>
> He will reap for 2 days with food as above and the service is worth 2*d*.
>
> His aforesaid services with plough-service as it pertains to him are worth 7*d*.
>
> He will give 18*d* as tallage.
>
> He will be reeve if elected and he will have [those benefits] as above.

Walter Attetouneshende, free in body, holds 1 ferling of land in Thorne; 5*s* 6*d* at the said terms.

> With the aforesaid Adam Baldewine he will plough for 1 day in winter and another day in Lent. His own service in this is worth 4½*d*.
>
> He will do hay-making for half a day and the work is worth ½*d*.
>
> He will reap for 2 days with food as above and the work is worth 2*d*.
>
> His services are worth 7*d*.
>
> He will give 4*d* as tallage.
>
> He will be reeve.

Thomas atte Shuete, free in body, holds 1 dwelling-house and 6 acres of land in Thorne; 3*s* at the said terms.

> He will plough for 1 day when the lady wishes with food as above and the work is worth 6*d*.

---

[15] There is a Simon Breghe listed under Ayshford in *DLS*, p. 40.

He will reap for 2 days with food as above and the work is worth 2*d*.

Thus his works are worth 7*d*.

He will give 6*d* as tallage.

He will be reeve.

John le Pottere of Chieflowman [*Chyldelomene*], villein, holds 1 ferling of land in Chieflowman; 5*s* 6*d* at the said terms.

> He will give 19¼*d* as tallage.
>
> For hearth-penny [*hertpeni*] he will give 1*d*.

Nicholas Ysaac,[16] villein, holds ½ ferling of land in Chieflowman; 5*s* 6*d* at the said terms.

> He will give 19¼*d* as tallage.
>
> For hearth-penny he will give 1*d*.

Robert Golde,[17] villein, holds ½ ferling of land in Chieflowman; 5*s* 6*s* at the said terms.

> He will give 19¼*d* as tallage.
>
> For hearth-penny he will give 1*d*.

William le Potter, villein, holds ½ ferling of land in Chieflowman; 5*s* 6*d* at the said terms.

> He will give 19¼*d* as tallage.
>
> For hearth-penny he will give 1*d*.

William Aluard, villein, holds ½ ferling of land in Chieflowman; 5*s* 6*d* at the said terms.

> He will give 19¼*d* as tallage.
>
> For hearth-penny he will give 1*d*.

Nicholas Megre, villein, of Wytheneth holds at will 1 dwelling-house and 5 acres of land in Lomene at Wytheneth; 3*s* at the said terms.

> He will give 12*d* as tallage.
>
> He will be reeve.

Richard atte Shuete, free in body, of Thorne holds at will 1 dwelling-house and 5 acres of land in Thorne; 4*s* at the said terms for all service.

> He will give nothing as tallage.
>
> He will not be reeve.

---

[16] This is a Nicholas Isaak listed under Chieflowman in *DLS*, p. 36.

[17] There is a Robert Golde listed under Chieflowman also in *DLS*, p. 36.

Rose Potter, free in body, of Smethenecote in the parish of Uffculme [*Ufculm*] holds at will 1 ferling of land; 4*s* at the said terms for all service.

Total rent of the free tenants £10 17s 5d from which the farm of the mill is 12s and 1 pound of wax.

Total rent of the tenants in bondage and at will £6 11s 10d from which in every term before the feast of Saint Michael [left blank] and in the term of Saint Michael [left blank].

Total value of their work [left blank].

Sum of the tallage 20s 4¼d, and of hearth-penny 5d.

Sum of the plough-service of the aforesaid tenants [left blank].

Sum of their other services, hoeing-services, mowing services, reaping services, services with beasts, carrying-services with wagon for gathering the hay, other carrying services for the bean stack, the cleaning of the mill-leat, hay-making, help with making the hay-cocks, help with the bean stacks, trenching for the corn etc, where it is understood to always be with 1 man etc. [left blank].

Total acres of meadow mown by the customary tenants [left blank]; on the allowance of their rent in the term of Saint John the Baptist [left blank].

Total of the works for the mowing of the meadow [left blank] for food of the lady as shown above [left blank].

Sum total of the rent £17 9s 3d and 1 pound of wax.

Note that for any of the aforesaid tenants at will, when he dies or gives up his tenement, he will give his best beast as heriot; if he is of the parish of Burlescombe he will make mortuary payment of his second-best beast after his death, together with his aforesaid heriot.

[The following note at the end of fol. 169v was added at a much later date in a more cursive, informal style]

> Joan the daughter and heir of Joan Chubbeworthy paid homage to the lady at
> Leigh on 21st day of the month [name is missing] in the second year of the reign
> of King Henry VI for the tenements that she holds in Thorne.[18]

---

[18]   There are some superscript characters between the words *pro* and *tenementa* that are hard to decipher. The second year of reign of Henry VI ran from 1 September 1423 to 31 August 1424.

Manor of Rockbeare

Extent of the manor of Rockbeare made on Tuesday after the feast of the nativity of John the Baptist [28 June] 1323, the third year of Margaret [Aunger] as abbess.

[Jurors who declare by oath]

William atte Wylle, Walter atte Pyle, Walter Elyote, Walter Bysouthewode, Henry atte Crosse and Henry Langeman.[1]

[Demesne land]

Arable. The arable acreages are in Penyacres 16 acres, Lomecopy 20 acres, Ludebroke 15½ acres, Buddesmere 20 acres, Kammokhille 2 acres, Buthepol 7 acres, Guuyldthorne 12 acres, Westhaye 15 acres, next to the rectory 15 acres, next to Ludebroke 12 acres, Lefdywille 6 acres, Byfarweye 9 acres 1 perch, in the close next to the court 15½ acres, next to the wood and meadow 12 acres, in Goteleghe 20 acres, and Attarhose 5 acres.

Sum of the acreages of arable 202 acres 1 perch. Value per acre 2*d*, thus in total 33*s* 8½*d*.

Meadowland. In Estparke 14½ acres, in Westparke 26½ acres. The price per acre is 12*d*.

Sum of the acreages of meadow 41 acres. The total value is 41*s* per annum.

Woodland. In Goteleghe 21 acres, in Westwode 6 acres.

The annual value per acre of pasture [*sic, should say woodland*] 2*d*.

Sum of the acreages of woodland 27 acres. They are worth in total per annum 4*s* 6*d*.

The court. In Pyrihey 2 acres. In the court and close 2 acres.

Sum of the acreages 4 acres. The value per annum is 2*s*.

The total value of the demesne land with the meadow, woodland and court is £4 14½d.

---

[1] All but Henry atte Crosse are listed under Rockbeare in *DLS*, p. 104. There is a Henry atte Crosse listed on p. 3, but his entry is under the manor of Ipplepen.

[Free tenants]

Warin de Hampton freeman by hereditary right holds by charter one tenement at La Rewe and five ferlings [*ferlingos*] of land, 1*d* at Easter for all service.[2]

The same Warin by hereditary right holds by charter at La Hose and La Forde 4 ferlings of land; 14*s* per annum in equal amounts at the feasts of Easter and of Saint Michael [29 September] and two suits of court, namely at La Hockeday and at the feast of St Michael.[3] He holds by military service.

Joel Puddyng holds at La Forde and La Hylle 7 ferlings of land by charter by hereditary right and by military service; 6*d* per annum at Easter for all service.

Peter atte Wode freeman holds by charter 2 ferlings of land at La Wode by military service; 1*d* per annum at Easter for all service.[4]

The total rents of the free tenants 14s 8d.

[Bonded tenants]

William atte Wille [*one of the jurors*], villein of the lady [*natiuus Domine*] holds in bondage 2 ferlings of land; 8*s* per annum at the four terms.[5]

> He must, if he has oxen, plough the winter-sown crop and the spring-sown crop at the will of the lady with food from the lady once in the day. The work is worth 7½*d* to the lady.
>
> He must perform harrowing for 1 day and will have lunch. The work is worth 1*d* to the lady.
>
> He must do hoeing/weeding [*sarculare*] for 1 day and will have lunch. The work is worth a halfpenny.
>
> He must make hay for 1 day and will have lunch once. The work is worth a halfpenny.
>
> He must help with the making of the hayrick for 1 day and will have food twice. And the work is worth 1*d* to the lady.
>
> He must do mowing for 1 day with 1 man and both will have lunch. And the work is worth 2*d* to the lady.
>
> He must reap 3 times with 1 man and both will have lunch. And the work is worth 3*d* to the lady.

---

[2] Warin de Hampton is listed under Rockbeare in *DLS*, p. 104. For a definition of ferling, see the Glossary.

[3] Hockday was the second Tuesday after Easter Sunday. It was a common term day when rent and dues were paid.

[4] Peter atte Wode is listed under Rockbeare in *DLS*, p. 104.

[5] William atte Wille is listed under Rockbeare in *DLS*, p. 104. The four terms of the year are typically Easter, the Nativity of John the Baptist (24 June), Michaelmas (29 September) and the Nativity of the Lord (25 December).

He must clean out the mill-leat when necessary with others of his neighbours for 1 day and will have food twice. And the work is worth 1*d*.

He must carry the millstone to the second purchaser [*secundo emptori*] with others of his neighbours with the lady's wagon and two of her oxen.[6]

Walter Elyote [*one of the jurors*], free in body [*liber corpore*] holds two tenements at Southwode and 2 ferlings of land; 8*s* per annum at the aforementioned terms. He will duplicate all the services of the aforementioned William and he will gain all the same items [*et percipiet eodem modo in omnibus*].

Walter Bysouthewode [*one of the jurors*], villein, holds 1 ferling of land; 5*s* per annum at the aforementioned terms. He will do all the same services as the afore-mentioned William.

Henry Langeman [*one of the jurors*], free in body, holds 1 tenement and 1 ferling of land; 5*s* per annum at the aforementioned terms. He will do all the same services as the aforementioned William.

Adam Bysouthewode, free in body, holds 1 tenement, 1 ferling of land, 1 close and 12 acres of land; 11*s* at the aforementioned terms. He will do all the same services as the aforementioned William and no more.[7]

Walter Attarpyle, free in body, holds 1 tenement and 2 ferlings of land; 10*s* at the afore-mentioned terms. He will do all the same services as the aforementioned William.[8]

Peter Ludebroke holds 1 tenement and 6 acres of land; 2*s* at the aforementioned terms. He will do all the same services as the aforementioned William except ploughing and harrowing and in addition he will do trenching [*et grapiabit*] for 3 entire days or other work that may be required of him.[9] On each day he will have a halfpenny for food. The work is worth 1½*d* to the lady.

Henry atte Crosse [*one of the jurors*] holds 1 cottage and 6 acres of land; 2*s* at the aforementioned terms. He will do all the same services as the aforementioned Peter.

Matilda Russel holds 1 cottage and 6 acres of land; 2*s* at the aforementioned terms. She will do all the same services as the aforementioned Peter.

Susanna in the Toune holds 1 cottage and 6 acres of land; 2*s* at the aforementioned terms. She will do all the same services as the aforementioned Peter.

---

[6]   The term *secundo emptori* is discussed in the Introduction.

[7]   Adam Bisouthwode is listed under Rockbeare in *DLS*, p. 104. There is a scribbled note in the right-hand margin next to the entry for Adam Bysouthewode that disappears off the right-hand edge of the folio. It appears to say *Item dictus grapiabit per .iij. dies et suf .j.d obolus*.

[8]   Walter atte Pille is listed under Rockbeare in *DLS*, p. 104.

[9]   *Grapiare* is a term not widely seen. Another example can be found at Historical Manuscripts Commission. 'Liber albus II: Fols. 63d–80'. *Calendar of the Manuscripts of the Dean and Chapter of Wells: Volume 1* (HMSO, 1907), British History Online. Web. 28 January 2025. https://www.british-history.ac.uk/wells-mss/vol1/pp336-352 (p. 347).

Philip Duc holds 1 cottage and 6 acres of land; 2s at the aforementioned terms. He will do all the same services as the aforementioned Peter.

John atte Barre holds 1 cottage and 6 acres of land; 2s 3d at the aforementioned terms. He will do all the same services as the aforementioned Peter.

Roger Bathe holds 1 cottage and 6 acres of land; 2s at the aforementioned terms. He will do all the same services as the aforementioned Peter.

Alice Parkere holds 1 cottage and 6 acres of land; 2s at the aforementioned terms. She will do all the same services as the aforementioned Peter.

Robert in the Toune holds 1 cottage and 1 acre of land; 21d at the aforementioned terms.[10]

> He will do hoeing for 1 day with food once in the day. The work is worth a halfpenny.
>
> He must do hay-making for 1 day with food. The work is worth a halfpenny.
>
> He must help with the making of the hayrick for 1 day and he will have food twice. The work is worth 1d.
>
> He must reap for 2 days with food from the lady. The work is worth 2d to the lady.
>
> He will clean out the mill-leat with others of his neighbours and will have food twice. The work is worth 1d to the lady.

William Walsch holds 1 house and 6 acres of land; 3s 4d at the aforementioned terms. He will do all the same services as the aforementioned Peter.[11]

Michael Rytoun holds 1 house and 6 acres of land; 3s 4d at the aforementioned terms. He will do all the same services as the aforementioned Peter.

Alice Attaroke holds 1 house and 2 acres of land; 2s at the aforementioned terms. She will do all the services of the aforementioned Robert in the Toune except for helping with the making of the hayrick and the cleaning of the mill-leat.

The total value of the rents of the villeins 73s 8d.

The total value of their services 18s 2½d.

The total value of the entire manor from the extent as it stands above £9 7s 9d.

---

[10] There are two entries for Robert in the Toune in *DLS* on pp. 47 and 65. However, they are for the distant manors of Kilmington and Tavistock respectively and thus are not likely to be this tenant.

[11] There are entries for a William Walshe in *DLS* on pp. 62 and 95. Again these are unlikely to be the Rockbeare tenant.

Note that whichever of the aforementioned tenants, if they hold two tenements and become the reeve, then their allowance as reeve will be just for one tenement. And such a tenant when they die will render heriot for both tenements.

Note that none of the above may have his son educated, nor arrange marriage for his daughter, nor sell a young male horse that has been foaled to him, nor an ox that has been calved to him, without permission of the ladies.

Note that any villein of the lady, whether holding land in the manor or not, if they have a draught animal then they will render a heriot when they die.

Note that this manor of Rockbeare is burdened with suit of court at the hundred of Ryngeswille, which is commonly redeemed for 4s.

And thus the manor, by means of the extent when the above burdens are deducted, is worth £9 3s 9d.

Note that the advowson of the church of the same manor belongs to the said abbey from the first gift of the countess of Gloucester. And the abbess and convent of the same place lately presented Master Gilbert Bydeford to that church who was recently inducted rector there.[12] And he was instituted in the same. And that advowson is not given a value because it does not accrue any annual profit.

Note that the aforementioned tenants say that Adam atte Hose, who held four ferlings at La Forde and La Hose in the same manor, held the same tenure for his lifetime by grant of Robert Burnel, formerly lord of the same manor.[13] Such is common knowledge in the neighbourhood. And at present that tenure is transferred from hand to hand. So that Warin de Hampton, now the tenant, claims to hold the same tenancy by inheritance for 14s thereupon in the manor, rendering such for all service except for two suits of court.

[What follows was added much later and in a different, more cursive hand]

Note that on the Monday next before the feast of St Martin in the eleventh year of the reign of King Henry IV John Faryngdon paid homage to Lucy abbess of Canonsleigh at Canonsleigh for the lands and tenements that he holds from the lady at Hose and Forde within the manor of Rockbeare.[14]

Note that Robert Bron paid his homage to the lady on the third day of July in the abovementioned year for the lands and tenements that he holds from the lady in Wode within the manor of Rockbeare.[15]

[12] There is a very brief entry for a Master Gilbert de Bideford in *BRUO*, i, p. 185.
[13] Robert Burnell was bishop of Bath and Wells between 1275 and 1292.
[14] The date equates to Monday, 4 November 1409. Lucy Warre was abbess from June 1370 to October 1410.
[15] Thursday, 3 July 1410.

Note that John Drake on 21st day of the month of October in the eighth year of the reign of Henry Sixth paid homage to the lady Mary, abbess of Canonsleigh, for the lands and tenements that he holds in Hose and Forde by right of his wife within the manor of Rockbeare.[16]

Note that John Storton paid homage to the lady for the lands and tenements that he holds in Hylle and Forde by right of his wife within the manor of Rockbeare by his letters patent [entry undated].[17]

[16] Friday, 21 October 1429. Mary Beauchamp was abbess from November 1410 until December 1449.

[17] That this entry is not dated and that the name of the abbess is not given raises some interesting questions. Was this entry added long after the event to provide authenticity to a disputed claim? Unfortunately, there are no surviving court records for the manor of Rockbeare.

MANOR OF DUNSFORD

[Donesford]

Extent of the manor of Dunsford made on Wednesday the feast of the apostles Peter and Paul, 1323,[1] the third year of Margaret [Aunger] as abbess.

[Jurors who declare by oath]

William Colebrygge, William de Bylonde, Robert de Colrygge, Roger atte Sele, Roger Smallake and John Walsch.[2]

[Free and unfree tenants]

Henry de Moulysch holds by hereditary right 5 ferlings of land at Byry; nothing to pay but he does suit of court whenever it is held. He will be the tithingman for the whole manor in perpetuity. He will always owe and find five pence and five men at all guild meetings [*ad omnes gulda*] and services of the lord king within the said manor. The lady will have wardship when he dies.

Alexander Feraunt, freeman, holds 3 ferlings by hereditary right for military service. And he must do suit of court as previously for all services.

William de la Forde, freeman, holds 2 ferlings of land by hereditary right in free socage [*libero socagio*]; 12s at the four terms of the year. He will do suit of court as above.

John le Tayllour and William de Boylonde [*juror*] hold 1 ferling of land in Boylonde in free socage; 6s at the aforementioned terms for all services except for suit of court as above.

The same John and William, freemen, hold 1 ferling of land in the same place; nothing to pay for military service. They will render feudal due when it falls due. The lady will have wardship and marriage right when it falls due [*sic, cum acciderit*].

Joan Uppeton holds 2 ferlings of land in Uppeton in bondage; 13s 11d at the aforementioned terms for all service except for suit of court whenever it is held. Note: all her works and services and those of all the other bonded persons that follow, are placed in the [total] value of pence under the heading of rent.

The same [*Joan*] holds 1 portion of demesne meadow; 2s per annum.

---

[1]   Wednesday, 29 June 1323 in the Julian Calendar.
[2]   All six jurors are also listed as tenants within this extent.

Roger atte Sele [*juror*], villein of the lady, holds 2 ferlings of land there; 13*s* 11*d* at the aforementioned terms and suit of court as above. And for a meadow 2*s* as above.

Matilda in the Toune holds 1½ ferlings of land there; 10*s* 6*d* and suit of court as above; also one portion of meadow, 4*s* 6*d* per annum; For pasture in Boderdounesmore 4*d* per annum.

Joan the widow of Stephen Uppeton, free in body, holds in bondage 3 closes of land; 5*s* 8*d* at the aforementioned terms and suit of court as above. Also for 1 portion of meadow 7*d*.

Walter Uppeton, villein, holds 1½ ferlings of land; 10*s* 5½*d* at the aforementioned terms; suit of court as above; also for 1 portion of meadow 12*d*.

Susan in the More, free in body, holds there 1½ ferlings of land; 10*s* 6*d* at the aforementioned terms and suit of court as above; also for 1 portion of meadow 18*d* per annum.

William Stoddon, villein of the lady, holds 1 ferling and 1 close; 8*s* 9½*d* at the aforementioned terms; suit of court as above; for a portion of meadow 12*d*.

Hugh Woldeslonde, villein, holds 1 ferling of land there; 7*s* 1*d* at the aforementioned terms; suit of court as above; for a portion of meadow 12*d*.

Robert Colrygge [*juror*], villein of the lady, holds there 1 ferling of land; 7*s* 1*d* at the aforementioned terms; suit of court as above.

William atte Sele, villein, holds there 1 ferling of land and 1 close; 8*s* 9*d* at the aforementioned terms; suit of court; for a portion of meadow 12*d* per annum.

William Colebrygge [*juror*], villein, holds there 1 ferling of land and 1 close; 8*s* 9*d* at the aforementioned terms; suit of court as above; for a portion of meadow 15*d*; for pasture in Boterdounesmore 4*d*.

Roger Smallake [*juror*], villein, holds 1 ferling of land; 7*s* 4*d* at the aforementioned terms; suit of court as above; for a portion of meadow 12*d*; for pasture in Boterdounesmore 4*d*.

Richard Wytheleghe, free in body, holds there 2 closes of land; 4*s* 7*d* at the aforementioned terms; suit of court as above; for a portion of meadow 18*d* per annum.

John Uppehill, villein, holds there 1 close of land; 23*d* at the aforementioned terms; for a portion of meadow 3*d* per annum; suit of court as above.

William Wormyscomb, villein, holds there 1 close; 2*s* at the aforementioned terms; suit of court.

Mazeline atte Touneshende, villein, holds 1 ferling of land and 1 close; 9*s* at the aforementioned terms; suit of court as above; for a portion of meadow 12*d*; for pasture in Boterdonesmore 4*d* per annum.

John Walsch [*juror*], free in body, holds for the term of his life 1 ferling of land; 5*s* 10*d* at the aforementioned terms; suit of court as above; for a portion of meadow 12*d* per annum; for pasture in Buterdonesmore 4*d*.

John Barlahille, villein, holds there ½ ferling of land and 1 close; 5*s* 1½*d* at the aforementioned terms; suit of court as above; for a portion of meadow 6*d*.

Gregory Braz, villein, holds there 1 close of land without a house; 20*d* at the aforementioned terms; suit of court as above.

Margery Attarbrygge holds 1 close of land without a house; 20*d* at the aforementioned terms; suit of court as above.

Robert Attarporche, villein, holds 1 close of land without a house; 20*d* at the aforementioned terms; suit of court as above.

Acelota Shurecombe holds ½ ferling of land there; 3*s* 8*d* at the aforementioned terms; suit of court as above; for a portion of meadow 6*d* per annum.

Note that all these aforementioned tenants except for John Walsch will be reeves if they are elected. Then they will be quit of their aforementioned rents if they hold 1 ferling or less of land. If they hold more than 1 ferling then they will only be quit for 1 ferling.

Note that all the aforementioned tenants and the cottars who follow will, if they have draught animals, render their best beast as heriot when they die. And also all those villeins of the manor, even if they do not hold land, if they have draught animals they will render a heriot as above. And even any of the said tenants, although they hold 2 ferlings of land, or 3, or 2 tenements, they will render just 1 heriot when they die.

[Cottars]

Nicholas le Tayllour holds 1 cottage; 18*d* at the aforementioned terms; suit of court as above.

Matilda Uppehille holds cottage; 12*d* at the aforementioned terms; suit of court as above.

Robert Attarporche holds 1 cottage with a curtilage; 2*s* 1*d* at the aforementioned terms; suit of court as above.

Geoffrey Laurentz holds 1 cottage with a curtilage; 2*s* at the aforementioned terms; suit of court as above.

Susan la Welle holds 1 cottage with a curtilage; 6d at the aforementioned terms; suit of court as above.

Hugh Swepere holds 1 cottage with a curtilage and 1 acre of land; 9d at the aforementioned terms; suit of court as above.

Margery atte Brygge holds 1 cottage and 1 curtilage; 17d at the aforementioned terms; suit of court as above.

Geoffrey Bogeweye holds 1 cottage with a curtilage; 2s per annum; suit of court as above.

John Lange holds 1 cottage with a curtilage; 9d per annum; suit of court as above.

John Tayllour holds for his lifetime 1 cottage with a curtilage; 8d per annum etc. [*sic*]

William Dyrkyn for 1 portion of meadow; 12d per annum.

Sum total of all the rents of the above, whether free or in bondage, £10 5s 2½d

[The following tenant appears at the very bottom of fol. 147r; this entry seems to be a later addition and is in a different hand]

Matilda atte Porche holds 1 cottage without a curtilage; 6d in the 18th year.[3]

[*Demesne land*]

7 acres of marsh that provide income of 14d per annum to the lady.

Total 14d.

12 acres of oak woodland with dependencies across the water [*dependentis ultra aquam*] that cannot be valued because it is reserved to sustain the lords of the manor with the acre worth 2d per annum.

Total 2s.

6 acres of waste land from which the lady derives profit when it is cultivated. And when it is not cultivated the people of the manor have it in common there for their beasts to water and to graze and for the communal way to take water. Then the acre is worth 1d per annum.

Total 6d.

Thus, by the extent above, the manor with its rents is worth £10 8s 10½d

---

[3] It seems very possible that the term '18th year' refers to the regnal year of King Edward II, who was on the throne when the extents were compiled. The eighteenth year of his reign began on 8 July 1324.

[*The parsonage*]

The extent of the possessions and lands there of the parsonage made in the year and day within.

[*The demesne of the parsonage*]

1½ ferlings of land containing 90 acres of arable land. The acre is worth per annum in total 1*d*.

Total acreage of arable land 90 acres; total value 7s 6d

3 acres of meadow, worth per acre per annum 12*d*.

Total 3s.

1 dovecot, worth 12*d*.

The court and garden worth 2*s*.

The church is taxed at the true value of 12 marks [*£8*].

Total value from the above extent £8 13s 6d

[*Tenants of the parsonage*]

William atte Broke, freeman, holds by charter by hereditary right; 3*s* at the four terms for all services as they [*the jurors*] believe; the lady will have wardship etc. when it occurs.

Philip French, free in body, holds 1 house and curtilage; 3*s* at the aforementioned terms. And suit of court etc.

Nicholas Tayllour holds 1 curtilage; 6*d* for all services.

William Derkyn, villein, holds 1 ferling of land; 6*s* 8*d* at the aforementioned terms; suit of court etc.

Henry Perkerygg, villein, holds ½ ferling of land; 3*s* 8*d* per annum; suit of court etc.

Geoffrey Kynelond holds ½ ferling of land; 3*s* 8*d*; suit of court.

Sum total of the rents of the parsonage, 20s 6d.

Thus the church is worth, with the rents of the tenants, its demesne land and meadow: £9 14s

Note that the aforementioned church was made payer of a pension [*pensionara*] to the church of St Peter of Exeter [*Exeter Cathedral*] for 53*s* 4*d* annually owing after tax, which deductions value the church with its appurtenances written above at £7 8*d*. Note that the aforesaid manor is burdened with suit of court at the hundred of Woneford which is normally bought off for 2*s* annually.

And thus the church with the manor is worth, by clear deduction with its obligations as written above, £17 7s 6½d

There is a free manor there with liberty from fine for the breach of assize of bread and ale, concerning the spillage of blood, from the right concerning the raising of hue and cry, and the raising of gallows and drowning-pool within the bounds of the same manor.[4] And the liberty is not included in the extent because its profit is transferred into the steward's expenses, as is regularly found in the account, nor elsewhere in the other manors of the abbey for the same reason.

[The following lines are a much later addition in a different hand]

Note that Richard Alforde and John Veer paid homage for lands and tenements in Boyland in the eighth year of the reign of King Henry IV etc.[5]

[The following entry at the bottom of fol. 147v is a much later addition in a different hand]

Roger Heurgoun and Philip Lanerdus paid homage to the lady at Legh for their lands and tenements in Dunsford on 20th day of March in the second year of the reign of King Henry VI.[6]

---

[4] The gallows were the punishment for male felons; for female felons, it was ordeal by drowning.
[5] Year eight of the reign of Henry IV ran from 30 September 1406 to 29 September 1407.
[6] Monday, 20 March 1424.

MANOR OF HOCKFORD

The extent and custumal of the manor of Hockford made by Robert Aleyn, John Carswille, William Louecleue, William atte Wille, John de Loscombe, Richard Pope, Richard Kyngeman, William atte Wode, Roger de Slotynbeare, Robert Slotynbeare, Robert Wouham, Richard le Yem and Philip de Slanycombe,[1] jurors, on the Sunday next after the feast of Saint John the Baptist in the year of our Lord 1323,[2] and the third year of lady Margaret [Aunger] as abbess, who say that…

[Tenants]

Henry Berneuille holds at will 2 ferlings of land from the parsonage [de personatu] there; 3s at will. Those who previously held the vicarage before the present vicar, lord John, used to pay 6s, holding it at will while each lived.

Richard Kyngeman, villein, holds 1 ferling of land; 3s per annum at the four terms.

> He will plough for the oats for 3 days if he has the oxen and he will have food once each day or 1d each day. The work is worth 5d to the lady.

> He will harrow if he has the draught animals provided that the plough tills for 1 day and he will have food or ½d. The work is worth ½d.

> He must hoe for half a day and he will have ½d. Thus it is worth nothing for the lady.

> He must mow for 1 day and will have lunch or 1½d. The work is worth 1½d to the lady.

> He must do hay-making for half a day and he will have nothing. The work is worth ½d.

> He must carry the hay of the lady with a wagon and oxen if he has oxen amounting to a full plough-team [ad plenam carucam] and he will have food twice and the work is worth 3d to the lady. If he does not have the full plough-team himself then with one other of his neighbours he is to do the same work.

> He must reap for 4 days with 1 man and will have lunch twice. The work is worth 4d to the lady.

> He must clean out the mill-leat with other neighbours of his. The work is worth ¼d.

> He must give ½d for the roofing of the hall when it will be necessary.

---

[1] Of the list of jurors, the following appear in DLS (p. 87) for the parish of Hockworthy: Robert Aleyn, John de Carswille, William de Loueclyue, John de Loscombe and Robert de Slotynbere. A William atte Wille appears on p. 104 at Rockbeare. There is a Richard Pope on p. 51 at Fursham. A William atte Wode appears on p. 36 at Uplowman.

[2] Sunday, 19 June 1323.

For the roofing of the grange he will give ½*d* when it will be necessary.

He, with others of his neighbours, must re-roof the mill at their own expense with the straw and bindings of the lady.

He must carry the millstone with his own oxen with other neighbours if he has oxen, with the wagon of the lady and 2 oxen.

He will repair the wall of the mill whenever it will be necessary with food from the lady twice in the day; the works are not valued because they occur rarely.

He will give 9*d* as tallage at the feast of Saint Michael.

He will be reeve if so elected. Then he will be quit of the said rent and afore-mentioned services.

Philip de Slanycombe, villein, holds 2 ferlings and 1 close of land; 6*s* 9*d* per annum at the four terms. And he will duplicate the services of the said Richard in all respects. He will give 20¼*d* as tallage. If he is elected he will be reeve; then he will be quit for 1 ferling of land as above.

John de Loscombe, villein, holds 2 ferlings of land there; 2*s* at the said terms. He will duplicate the services of the said Richard in all respects. He will give tallage of 18¼*d*. If elected he will be reeve as stated above.

Nicholas Pope, villein, holds 2 ferlings of land at Dyrisleghe; 6*s* at the aforesaid terms.[3] He will duplicate the services of the said Richard in all respects. He will give 18*d* as tallage. He will be reeve as above.

William atte Wode, villein, holds 1½ ferlings of land; 4*s* 6*d* at the aforesaid terms. And he will perform the services for 1 ferling of land as the aforesaid Richard. And for the works of half a ferling he will give 8*d*. And he will give tallage of 13½*d*. He will be reeve as above.

Roger Slotyngbeare, villein, holds 1 ferling of land; 3*s* at the aforesaid terms. He will do all services as the aforesaid Richard Kyngeman and will 9*d* as tallage. He will be reeve as above.

Robert Slotyngbeare, villein, holds 2 ferlings of land; 6*s* at the aforesaid terms. He will duplicate the services of the aforesaid Richard Kyngeman in all respects. He pays 18*d* as tallage. He will be reeve as above.

Robert de Wougham, villein, holds 2½ ferlings of land; 7*s* 6*d* at the aforesaid terms. He will duplicate the services of the said Richard for 2 ferlings. For half a ferling he will do no work. He pays 22½*d* as tallage. He will be reeve as above.

Nicholas de Wougham, villein, holds 2 ferlings and 1 close of land; 6*s* 9*d* at the aforesaid terms. He will do the services for 1 ferling of land as the aforesaid Richard Kyngeman. He pays 20¼*d* as tallage. He will be reeve as above.

---

[3]   There is a Nicholas Pope listed in *DLS* under the parish of Hockworthy (p. 87). The manor of Hockford is within that parish.

Robert Aleyn, free in body, holds 2 ferlings and 1 close of land; 6s 9d at the aforesaid terms. He will duplicate the services of the aforesaid Richard Kyngeman. He pays 20¼d as tallage. He will be reeve as above.

John Carswylle, free in body, holds 3 ferlings of land; 9s at the aforesaid terms. He will do the services for 2 ferlings of land then. He pays 2s 3d as tallage. He will be reeve as above.

William Louecleue, villein, holds 2½ ferlings of land; 7s 6d at the aforesaid terms. He will do the services for 1 ferling of land just as the aforesaid Richard. He pays 22½d as tallage. He will be reeve as above

William atte Wylle, villein, holds 1 ferling of land; 3s at the aforesaid terms. He will do the services as the aforesaid Richard Kyngeman. He pays 9d as tallage. He will be reeve as above.

Richard le Yem, villein, holds 1 ferling and 1 close of land; 3s 9d per annum. He will do services as the aforesaid Richard Kyngeman. He pays 11¼d as tallage. He will be reeve as above.

Note that whoever holds 2 ferlings or more, if he has a plough he will only do 1 plough-service. If 2 tenants hold 2 ferlings, namely each 1 ferling, they will plough with their oxen jointly, each will be quit for one plough-service.

[Cottars]

Alexander Palmere holds 1 cottage with a curtilage;[4] 12d per annum for all services.

Philip Durlyng holds 1 cottage and 1 close of land; 14d per annum for all services. He pays 2¼d as tallage at the feast of Saint Michael.

Matilda atte Wylle holds 1 cottage and curtilage; 12d per annum for all services.

Maurice de Slotyngbeare holds 1 cottage and curtilage; 12d per annum for all services.

Joan Pope holds 1 cottage and curtilage; 12d per annum for all services.

Roger Slotyngbeare holds 1 cottage and curtilage; 12d per annum for all services.

Joan Intheheye holds 1 cottage and curtilage; 12d per annum for all services.

Roger Slotyngbeare, for ½ acre next to the wood and a small plot there, 10 hens or 20d.

William Pope for the park of Lauehenede, 12 hens or 2s.

---

[4] There is an Alexander le Palmer under Hockworthy in DLS (p. 87).

Robert Aleyn and Richard le Yem for some pasture, 5 hens or 10*d*.

Note that the manor is burdened with the annual rent of 4*s* owing at the feasts of Saint Michael and Easter to Henry de Berneuile. Also 2¼*d* at the periodical court of the sheriff [*ad turnum vicecomitis*].

Also for the hundred court of Bampton a fine of 40*d* by custom.

Sum total of rent £4 14s 2d with 6s of rent from Waterslade as it was accustomed to pay. Where only 3s are placed in the account as now in rent.

Sum of the tallage at the feast of Saint Michael 19s 10½d (2¼d from the cottars).

Total value of all the works 25s 3¾d.
    Sum of the mowing works, 21 [sic]⁵
    Sum of the hay-making works 21
    Of the carriage of the hay 21
    Sum of the reaping work 84
    For the help in cleaning the mill-leat 21

Note that none of the aforementioned tenants in bondage may have their son educated nor see their daughter married, nor sell their male horse, colt, ox or calf, without the permission of the ladies. When any of them dies or gives up their tenement, he will give his best beast to the ladies as heriot.

[*Arable land*]

[The extent ends rather abruptly here]

---

5 The scribe did not include the monetary denomination here – it should be pence (*denarii*).

MANOR OF NETHERTON

[*Nytherton*]

The extent of the manor of Netherton made in that place on Monday after the feast of the Nativity of St John the Baptist,[1] in the year of the lord 1323 and in the third [year] of the blessing of the lady Margaret [Aunger], abbess. By the oath of Ralph Davy, John Matheu, John in the Huyrne, Nicholas Matheu, Henry Pouke and Thomas Clanfeld, who say on their oath:

[*Demesne*]

[*Arable land*]

In the Estfeld 45 acres.
In Myddelfeld with Chelfhamcrofte 43 acres.
In Westfeld 45 acres.

The sum of the acres of arable land is 133 acres.
The acre is worth 3d. And thus in total 33s 3d.

[*Waste land*]

There are 12 acres of waste land there next to Cnolhouse.
6 acres next Bromlegh'.

The sum of the acres of waste land is 18 acres.
The acre is worth 2d and thus in total 3s.

[*Meadow*]

There is meadowland there namely in Pynnoweshele 1 acre.

At Wodham 1 acre.
At Bromleghe 2½ acres.
At Coweswode 3 acres.
At Broclond 1 acre.
At Worthy 1 acre.
At Holemede 1 acre 1 perch.
At la Deremede 2½ acres 1 perch.
In la Hamme 1½ acres 1 perch.
In Crofte 1½ acres 1 perch ~ whereof 2 acres are only mown every other year.

---

[1] This feast was celebrated on 24 June. The following Monday in 1323 was on 27 June.

The sum of the acres of meadow is 17 acres and the acre is worth 12d except for the aforementioned 2 acres that are not mown that do not fall within the extent.
Thus in total 16s.

[*Alder wood*]

At Bromlegh 3 acres.
In la Hammes 4 acres.
The acre is worth 3*d* per year.

The sum of the acres of woodland is 7 acres and the acre is worth 3d.
Thus in total 21d.

[*The court house*]

Also the court house with adjoining close [comprises] 2 acres. And the acre is worth 3*d*.

Sum 6d.

[*Common pasture*]

There are 60 acres on the hills that lie as common pasture. And it is not given a valuation because it lies as common pasture. Nor is there another profit in respect of any common pasture.

[*Dovecot*]

1 dovecot there is worth 12*d* per year.

[*Mill*]

A mill there is generally worth 24*s* per year.

The sum of the value of the demesne land with meadow, the dovecot and mill [is]
79s 6d.

[*Tenants*]

The heirs of Jordan of Wyteleghe for 1½ acres of meadow in Langemede; ½*d*, due at Easter.[2]

The heirs of Thomas de Bromleghe for the land of Putteley and Wytheham; 2*d* owing at the feasts of the Nativity of St John the Baptist and of St Michael from the gift of William le Harper as is clear in his charter at number X.[3]

---

[2]   Whitley (Witheleghe, Wyteleghe) lay in the parish of Farway (*Cartulary*, p. xxvii).
[3]   See *Cartulary*, item 164 (p. 60).

William de Clanefelde holds 2 ferlings[4] of land there for the term of his life and Joan his wife by charter for which they pay annually at three fixed dates 8s 10½d, namely at the feasts of the Nativity of the Lord, Easter and St Michael in equal portions besides suit of court, and he will pay tax in common amercements with the bonded tenants.[5]

Simon Deveneys holds 1 ferling of land there for the term of his life; 5s per year for all services besides suit of court.

Roger Stowey freeman holds 1 ferling of land and 1 tenement at Stoweye in hered-itary fee; 2s 6d per year at the three aforementioned terms for all services besides suit of court, and save for service to the king (however much should pertain to land of such size).

Joan Deveneys holds by charter 1 ferling of land for the term of her life; 5s 3d at the aforementioned terms.

> If she has the oxen she will plough with food for 2 days as boon work. And the work is worth 6d.
>
> She must reap with 1 man for 4 days as boon work and to have dinner,[6] and the work is worth 6d to the Lady.
>
> She must help with the stacking of the hay and the work is worth ½d.
>
> She pays as tallage 2s 1d.

John Pouke, a villein of the Lady, holds 1 ferling of land at Poukehegh'; 3s per year at the aforementioned terms.

> He will plough half an acre of the winter crop and half an acre of the spring-sown crop and he will harrow without food. And the work with the harrowing is worth 6½d to the Lady.
>
> He will plough for 1 day in winter and for 1 other day in Lent as boon work. And he will have dinner once per day if he has the oxen. And the work is worth 6d.
>
> He will harrow once for the winter crop as boon work and he will have dinner, and once as boon work for the spring-sown crop and he will have dinner if he has draught animals. And the work is worth 1d to the Lady.
>
> He will harrow half an acre as is the custom and the work is worth ½d to the Lady.
>
> He must mow 1 acre of meadow without food and the work is worth 3d to the Lady.

---

[4]   A ferling is usually (though not always) defined as a quarter of a virgate. The definition of a virgate can also vary but is often given as 30 acres (P. D. A. Harvey, *Manorial Records, Archives and the User*, 5, rev. edn (British Records Association, 1999), p. 17). Thus a ferling in this context is probably about 7.5 acres. In this manuscript, the surveyor does not provide any clear definition for the term.

[5]   An amercement is a financial penalty levied by a court (Bailey, *The English Manor*, p. 241).

[6]   Boon-service or bond-service was compulsory labour provided without payment. It was seasonal in nature (Bailey, *The English Manor*, pp. 30, 241).

He will do hay-making for 2 half-days with 1 man and the work is worth ¾d to the Lady.

He will turn the hay or he will help with the stacking of the hay without food for half a day and the work is worth ½d.

He will reap 12 acres without food and the work is worth 3s to the Lady.

He will reap for 4 harvest services with 1 man, with food twice in the day. And the work is worth 5d to the Lady.

He will provide 4 carrying services with 1 man and with his draught animal per year, and at such a distance that he would be able on the next day to return home. And the work is worth 6d. And when he will come to Legh' he will have food.

Every week for 40 weeks he will labour at 1 item of work for half a day without food, and the work is worth 20d in total to the Lady, namely whatever task on whatever day ½d.

With others of his neighbours he will carry a millstone to the third purchaser.[7] And the Lady will provide the wagon and 2 oxen with 1 servant. And the afore-mentioned works are worth in total 7s 1¼d.

He will give 2s 1d as tallage after the feast of St Michael.

If the Lady so wishes he will clean out the mill-leat [bedum] with others of his neighbours.[8] And he will have ¾d. And thus it is worth nothing to the Lady.

He will be the reeve.

Henry Pouke, free in body, holds 1 ferling of land there; 3s at the aforementioned terms.

He will perform all the aforementioned services that the said John does.

He will benefit [percipiet] in the same way.

He pays 2s 1d for tallage.

John atte Hurne, free in body, holds half a ferling of land and botlonde; 2s 1½d at the aforementioned terms.[9]

He performs all the same services as the said John Pouke except that he only performs 2 carrying services.

He pays 12½d for tallage.

John Matheu, free in body, holds half a ferling of land; 18d at the aforementioned terms.

He performs all the same services as the said John atte Hurne.

He pays 12½d as tallage.

---

[7] This curious term is discussed in the Introduction.
[8] *Bedum* is normally translated as the mill-dam or mill-pond, but in this circumstance it probably refers more specifically to the mill-leat.
[9] The term *botlonde* here may be a variation on bond-land (land held by bondage tenure).

Ralph Davy, free in body, holds 1 ferling of land paying 5s at the aforementioned terms.

> He will plough half an acre for the winter crop and half an acre for the spring-sown crop and he will harrow without food. And the work is worth 6½d to the Lady.

> He will plough for 2 days as boon-service with food if he has the oxen. And the work is worth 6d to the Lady.

> He will harrow for 2 days as boon-service if he has the draught animals and he will have dinner. And the work is worth 1d.

> He will harrow as is customary without food and the work is worth ½d.

> He will reap for 4 days with 1 man and he will have dinner twice in the day. And the work is worth 5d to the Lady.

> He will help with stacking the hay and the work is worth ½d.

> He will clean the mill-leat with other neighbours as said previously.

> He will carry the millstone with other neighbours of his as above.

> He pays 2s 1d as tallage.

Nicholas Matheu holds 1 tenement and 6 acres of land; 18d at the aforementioned terms.

> He will plough for 2 days as boon-service if he has the oxen. And he will have dinner and the work is worth 6d.

> He will reap for 4 days with 1 man and he will have dinner. And the work is worth 6d to the Lady.

> He will harrow for 2 days as boon-service if he has the draught animals and he will have dinner and the work is worth 1d to the Lady.

> He will harrow half an acre by legal right and the work is worth ½d.

> He will help with the stacking of the hay and the work is worth ½d.

> He will help with the mill-leat and carrying the mill stone as above.

> He pays 6¼d as aid/tallage.

And it is understood that any of the aforementioned people in bondage will be the reeve if he be elected. And then he will be quit of all his rents and services. He may not educate his son nor give his daughter in marriage nor sell a young male horse that has been foaled to him or an ox that has been calved to him without permission of the Ladies.[10]

[Cottars]

Thomas Clanefelde holds 1 cottage and 1 acre of land and half an acre of meadow; 2s 3d per year.

---

[10] For a very similar passage, see *Custumals of the Manors of Laughton, Willingdon, and Goring*, ed. by A. E. Wilson, Sussex Record Society Publications, 60 (Sussex Record Society, 1961), p. 71.

He will reap 1 acre. And the work is worth 3*d*.

He will help with the stacking of the hay and the work is worth ½*d*.

He pays 1¾*d* as tallage.

Geoffrey Rinel holds 1 cottage and 1 acre of land; 12*d* per year.

He will reap 1 acre of land and the work is worth 3*d*.

He will help with the stacking of the hay and the work is worth ½*d*.

He pays 2¼*d* as tallage.

Philip Kymer holds 1 cottage with a curtilage; 15*d* per year.

He will reap 1 acre and the work is worth 3*d*.

He will help with the stacking of the hay and the work is worth ½*d*.

He pays 1*d* as tallage.

Matilda Turnour holds 1 cottage with a curtilage; 15*d* per year for all services.

Agnes the widow of the smith holds 1 cottage and 1 acre of land; 2*s* 3*d* per year.

She will reap 1 acre. And the work is worth 3*d*.

She pays 1½*d* as tallage.

Robert Turnour holds 1 cottage with a curtilage; 18*d* per year.

He will reap 1 acre. And the work is worth 3*d*.

* Richard Spynke holds 1 cottage; 12*d* per year.

He will reap 1 acre and the work is worth 3*d*.

* John Faber [Smith] holds 1 tenement with half an acre of meadow; 3*s* per year for all services.

Alice Couple holds 1 cottage; 12*d* per year.

She will reap 1 acre. And the work is worth 3*d*.

William atte Hurne holds 1 cottage with a curtilage; 15*d* per year for all services.

Walter Batyn holds 1 cottage and 2 acres; 3*s* 6*d* per year.

He will reap 1 acre. And the work is worth 3*d*.

The Pypere tenement that used to yield 15*d* for all services is in the hand of the Lady.

The curtilage of the smith that Roger Smith [*Faber*] used to hold and which used to yield 9*d* for all services, is in the hand of the Lady.

The sum of all the rent whether of freemen or of villeins [is] 61s ½d.

The sum of the tallage of the villeins there [is] 12s.

The sum of the value of the services and works of the said tenantry if they have oxen is 34s 8d.

The sum of the total value of the demesne in the aforementioned extent £9 7s 2½d.

Note that in this manor there is 2½d in deficit that the heirs of Thomas de Bromleghe and the heirs of Jordan de Wyteleghe ought to pay, as is certainly evident through the charters for Netherton at numbers X and XI.[11]

Note that this manor is burdened with suit of court at the hundred of Colyton which is normally redeemed for 3s 4d annually.

The aforementioned manor is burdened with 1 pound of wax usually priced at 7d, and of 4d, owing annually to the Abbot of Quarr[12] and to John of Pultymor for the land of Swetrygge and the common on the land of Wyteleghe as is certainly evident through the charter of Roger of Pultimor at number V.[13]

[The abbey] is burdened with 1d of annual rent owing on the feast of Saint Michael to the lords of Colewylle, as is certainly evident through the charter of William de Colewille at number III.[14]

Also it is burdened with the royal service named Horderisyne annually for 1½d.[15]

And thus the manor, with all the aforementioned burdens deducted, is worth, net, £9 2s 7½d in the aforementioned extent.

[The following entries concerning homage were added later by a different hand]

Note that on the Monday following the feast of St Martin in the eleventh year of the reign of King Henry IV,[16] John the son and heir of Agnes Hurne made his homage to Lucy the abbess of Canonleghe at Canonleghe for the tenements that he holds from the Lady in Stowey as from her manor of Netherton.

---

[11] *Cartulary*, items 164 and 165 on pp. 60–1.
[12] The Cistercian Abbey of Quarr was founded in the first half of the twelfth century on the Isle of Wight (Knowles, *Medieval Religious Houses*, p. 113). Some lands held of Quarr had been granted to the canons when they were resident at Canonsleigh (*Cartulary*, items 159 and 182).
[13] *Cartulary*, item 159, pp. 58–9. Poltimore lay in the parish of Farway (*Cartulary*, p. xxvii).
[14] *Cartulary*, item 157, p. 58. The lands of Colwell lay in the parish of Farway (ibid., p. xxvii).
[15] For definition of a similar term once used in Devon (horderesgeve), see R. E. Latham, 'Curia Tremure', *The English Historical Review* 71 (1956), pp. 428–33 (p. 431) where he discusses the meaning of 'horders gift'.
[16] This would equate to Monday, 4 November 1409. The lengthy abbacy of Lucy Warr ended with her death on 11 October 1410 (see *Cartulary*, p. 117 for the list of abbesses; also Smith and London, pp. 549–50; David M. Smith, *The Heads of Religious Houses England and Wales: 3, 1377–1540* (Cambridge University Press, 2008), pp. 634–5).

Also Richard Hurne made homage there to the Lady Joan Arundelle Abbess of Canonleghe for the lands and tenements aforementioned, on the tenth day of November in the sixth year of the reign of King Edward IV.[17]

Also William Russelle made his homage there to the Lady Elizabeth Fouhelle Abbess of Canonsleigh for the lands and tenements called Stowey that he holds from the Lady from the aforementioned manor, on the twelfth day of November in the nineteenth year of the reign of King Henry VII.[18]

[17] Monday, 10 November 1466.
[18] Sunday, 12 November 1503. Elizabeth Fowell was the very last abbess of Canonsleigh – her abbacy continued until the dissolution in February 1539.

MANOR OF SAMPFORD ARUNDEL

[*Saunford Arundel*]

The extent of the possessions and lands of the abbess and convent of Legh of the canonesses in Sampford Arundel, made on the day and year written above.[1]

[*Arable land*]

In Staberlond 42½ acres; in Langeslade above the grange there 14½ acres 1 rod; in Dygeleshille 3½ acres; above la Holebemes 3½ acres of arable land, price per acre 4*d*.

The total number of acres of arable land is 64 acres 1 rod with a value as above
Thus in total the overall value is 21s 5d, namely 4d per acre.

[*Moorland*]

Beneath Dygeleshille are 4 acres 1 rod. The value per acre as above is 4*d*.

Total 4 acres 1 rod. Total value 17d.

There is common pasture in Sampford pertaining to the tenants of the ladies where the rearing of any number of animals [*sine numero*] upon Blackdown [*Blakedoune*] is permitted;[2] it is not given a value because purchasers thence would not be able to determine it.

The church of the village of Sampford remains appropriated to the ladies and is assessed at the fair value of 7 marks.[3]

[*Farm of the mill*]

There is a mill there that is given over at farm to Benedict Collebon for 10*s* payable at the four terms in equal portions; he will provide for all the upkeep of the mill there and its mill-pond. However the lady abbess will provide the timber for that same place when it is needed and will provide carriage for it to the said mill. The lady herself will undertake carriage of the millstones to the said mill, but the farmer himself will meet the costs of them.

[*Tenants*]

Roger Frankelyn holds at will in Sampford from the said lady 1 acre of land without

---

[1] The date referred to is that given for the home manor of Leigh, namely Sunday, 12 June 1323.
[2] This is possibly the first reference to the name Blackdown in the medieval sources.
[3] A mark was worth two-thirds of a pound, i.e. 13*s* 4*d*.

a house next to Bembrygge;[4] 6d at the said terms for all services except for suit of court at Leigh.

Richard Coleman holds in Sampford 1 acre of land without a house called Stonacre; 10d at the aforementioned terms for all services except for suit of court as above.

George Collebon holds 1 house with a croft and curtilage; 3s at the four terms and must do suit of court as above.

Sum total of all rents together with the farm of the mill 14s 4d, whence from the farm 10s etc. [sic]

The total of the aforementioned value with the rents and the mill from the above extent £6 10s 6d with the church

Note that the vicar benefits from all obventions and oblations and all of the small tithes.[5] Also the tithes of the curtilage and of any similar kind. And the tithes of the hay will be provided from the meadows of Stephen de Bosco, Thomas de la Doune and Roger Frankelyn. Also 3 acres of arable land, 2 quarters of wheat and 2 of rye, 2 quarters of large oat [*grosse avene*] and 1 quarter of small oats [*minute avene*], 1 bushel of beans, 1 bushel of peas and the tithe of the mill. And he will secure the aforementioned corn in proportion at the four annual terms according to the ordinances of the vicarage as is stated in the charters of the ladies of Sampford at number 119.[6]

---

[4]   This name continues in use as Beambridge in the north of the manor.

[5]   All ecclesiastical fees and offerings; the small tithes were those due to the vicar, while the great tithes went to the rector (in this case, the abbess and convent as the church of Sampford Arundel was appropriated to them).

[6]   For item 119 of the charters, see *Cartulary*, pp. 42–3. The Latin text reads *super numerum I.I.IX*. This is the scribe's method for displaying an arabic number using roman numerals.

MANOR OF NORTHLEIGH

[*Northleghe*]

The extent of the manor of Northleigh, made on Monday next after the feast of the Nativity of Saint John the Baptist in the year of our Lord 1323 and the third year of Margaret [Aunger] as abbess,[1] by the oath of Henry Bubecnolle, William Jobbe, William Cok and John Leg.[2]

[*The demesne*]

[*Arable land*]

The arable lands in that place are in the South Field [*Campo Australi*] next to Wytemor 11½ acres, in Middle Field [*Middelfeld*] 15 acres, in North Field [*Northfeld*] 14 acres.

Total 40½ acres, price per acre 2d.
Total value 6s 9d.

[*Meadows*]

At Langemede 2 ½ acres; Hoberdesmille 1 acre; next to Wodemille 2 acres; next to Chelsham 1 acre; next to la Pounde 2 acres.

Total 8½ acres of meadow, price per acre 12d.
Total value 8s 6d.

[*Alder wood*]

At Tilcombe 6 acres; at Karlslynche 1 acre; at Wytemore ½ acre; next to Bubecnolle ½ acre.

Total 8 acres, price per acre 3d.
Total value 2s.

There is a certain plot at Hoberdesmille that was once built and used to pay 12d per annum in previous times and is now in the hand of the lady.

Total 12d.

Above Bromcnolle 1 acre of broom-land, value per annum 1d.

---

[1] Monday, 27 June 1323.
[2] There are several instances of William Cok listed in *DLS*, although none are definite 'hits'.

The close of the court contains 1 acre and the pasture of the same is commonly sold for 8*d*.

Total 8d.

Sum total value of the demesne land with meadow and the close of the court 19s.

Felicity de Bubecnolle, villein, hold half an acre of land; 2*s* per annum at the four terms.

She will plough 1 acre of the winter-sown crop without food, the work is worth 5*d*.

She will plough 1 acre of the spring-sown crop without food and the work is worth 5*d*.

If she does not have the oxen then she will give the aforementioned price.

She will hoe with two men for 3 days or she will give ¾*d*.

She will mow 5 acres of meadow and for that she will have 10*d*. And thus the work is worth 5*d*.

She will provide two servants on each day while she does hay-making for half a day, and the work of them is worth ½*d* per day, and in total 1½*d*.

If the lady will require the hay to be made up into bales [*fecerit leuare pratum ad pokes*] it will not be required in addition to help making the hayricks from the same, nor is it required therefore to carry nor turn the hay.

She will provide two servants for making the hay-cocks for 1 day and they will have food twice in the day. The work is not given a value because it is not worth the deduction from profits.

She should reap 12 acres and she will have nothing. The work is worth 3*s* to the lady.

She will reap whatever kind of corn and she will tie and stack in the field except for peas and such crops which she will reap but neither tie nor stack.

She will certainly not reap beans nor tie nor stack them.

She will reap for 6 days with 1 servant with food once in the day and she and the servant will come to their work at sunrise and will cease at sunset.

If she does not reap then she will give the lady 6*d*.

She will perform 14 works for 14 half-days from the feast of St Michael until the Nativity of the Lord. The work is worth 6½*d*.

Between the Epiphany of the Lord [6 January] and the Annunciation of the Blessed Virgin [25 March] 11 works for 11 half-days, price 6½*d*.

From the said feast until the Nativity of Saint John the Baptist [24 June] 11 works for 11 half-days, price 6½*d*.

For the rest of the time she will perform her aforementioned autumnal works.

And she will perform carrying-service four times in the year with 1 man and her draught horse when the lady requires it. When she does carrying-service she will have ½*d* or a meal once. The work is worth 6*d* to the lady.

She will do the carrying-service for 15 miles [*leucas*].

She will render tallage of 6*d*.

If the tenant should be a man then he will be the reeve if elected. Then he will be quit of the aforesaid rent and works.[3]

Thus the works written down above are worth 7*s* ¾*d*.

Joan Prate holds ½ ferling of land and 1 close; 5*s* per annum at the aforesaid terms.

She will hoe for 3 half-days or give ¾*d*.

She will do hay-making with one man in just the same manner as the said Felicity. The work is worth ¼*d* per day for at least 3 days.

She will help with the making of the hay-cocks with 1 man per day with food. The work is not given value for the aforementioned reason.

And she will reap for 3 days with 1 man with food once in the day or she will give the lady 3*d*.

She will give 15*d* as tallage.

The works of the aforesaid Joan are worth 4½*d*.

If the tenant is a man he will be elected reeve. Then he will be quit of all the aforesaid rent and services.

As boon work she should plough the winter-sown crop and the spring-sown crop if she has the oxen and she will have food. If she does not have oxen then she will not plough, nor will she give anything for plough-service.

John Legh holds 6 acres of land and 1 tenement; 2*s* at the aforesaid terms.

He will perform all the services as the said Joan except that he will not be reeve.

He will give 6*s* as tallage.

The works of the said John are worth 4½*d*.

William Cok holds 1 plot of land without a house; 3*s* 4*d* per annum at the terms aforesaid.

He will reap for 1 day and the work is worth 1*d*. Total value 1*d*.

Henry Bubecnolle holds 1 cottage with a curtilage; 2*s* at the aforesaid terms.

He will do all the same services as the aforementioned John except reeve service. His works are worth 4½*d*.

William Jobbe holds 1 house and 3 acres of land; 2*s* at the aforesaid terms for all services.

Sum total of rent, 16s 4d.
Total tallage, 2s 3d.
Sum of the value of the aforesaid services, 8s 2¼d.

---

[3]   Clearly a woman cannot be elected reeve. However, the surveyor is keen to emphasise that any successive male holder of this tenancy is eligible for election.

Sum total value of the manor as from the extent above, 45s 9¼d.

The manor is burdened with the annual payment to Nicola de Mortesthorne for her dower of the said manor of 19s 1d for her life. And to lady Petronilla de Kareute at whose request the said manor was the perquisite of the said abbey, 40s for the lifetime of the said lady Petronilla.

And thus the burden of the said manor exceeds the aforesaid value by 13s 3¾d.

Note that the advowson of the church of Northleigh pertains to the abbey of Leigh from the first gift of the Count of Gloucester of the same manor to the very same abbey during his life – when that happened to this point is uncertain. But it is commonly said that the abbess should by law present at the next vacancy. And this advowson is not given a value because it does not produce an annual profit for the said abbey.

THE EXTENTS SECTION B

THE EASTERN COUNTIES

MANOR OF SHEDDON

[*Schydyngho*]

The extent, rental and custumal made in that place on Tuesday, the vigil of Saint Laurence the Martyr in the seventeenth year of the reign of King Edward, son of King Edward, the third year of lady Margaret [Aunger] as abbess.[1] Homage rendered by all there.[2]

[*Free tenants*]

Richard de Buxton holds 1 tenement with curtilage and 3 acres of land adjoining in Sheddon. Also 1 plot in the marsh; 2*s* at the usual four terms of the year; 1*d* at the feast of Easter for the marsh; he must do suit of court every third week. He owes wardship, marriage-right, feudal relief and heriot when they fall due. And the lady abbess is seized of the wardship and marriage-right on account of his minority.[3]

The same Richard holds 1 garden and all of that land that William Batyn held from the gift of S. the clerk;[4] 4*s* at the four aforementioned terms. And he must do suit of court, wardship, marriage-right, feudal relief and heriot as above, from which the lady abbess is seized as above.

The same Richard holds certain land called Wrabbeslonde there; 8*d* at the said terms.

Thomas le Gros holds 1 plot of land that was sometime part of the land of Katherine Slyp under the wood of the hall [*sub bosco aule*];[5] 12*d* at the said terms. Suit of court, wardship, marriage-right, heriot and feudal relief when they fall due.

Agnes le Mulner holds another plot of land there that was Katherine's; 12*d* per annum. All services that the said Thomas does as above.

William Adam at La Forde holds 1 tenement and 40 acres of land by military service; 12*d* at the said terms. Heriot at his death.

The same William holds 2 acres of land in Fenlaunde; 2*d* at the said terms.

---

[1] Tuesday, 9 August 1323.
[2] Meaning all the tenants there. There is no separate list of jurors.
[3] Seisin simply means possession of a resource such as land.
[4] In the manuscript, the letter 'S' is not expanded, so it could mean a first name such as Stephen. Among the lands of William Batyn, there was a property called Prestesfeld (*Cartulary*, 239).
[5] Thomas and Katherine both feature in the extent for Manningtree. Of the forty-six names that appear in the Sheddon extent, twenty-four can also be found in the Manningtree extent.

The same William holds 1 piece of land that was Campion's; 6d at the said terms. William de Herkestede holds 1 tenement there that was Richard de Herkestede's and 5 acres of land; 6s at the said terms. Suit of court twice in the year. And suit of court twice in the year.[6] Wardship, feudal relief and heriot when they fall due.

John Gernoun holds 1 tenement there called Colettelonde; 2s per annum at the said terms from whence Christine la Dighe owes 5d and Bartholomew Tayllour 6½d. Suit of court, wardship, marriage-right, feudal relief and heriot when they fall due.

The same [John Gernoun] holds land that was Thomas LeReue's; 5s per annum at the said terms. And he does suit of court. And the lady will have wardship, marriage-right, feudal relief and heriot when they fall due.

The same holds a certain croft called Pykefeld; 16d at the said terms.

The same holds a land called Kebbeleslonde; 12d at the said terms as above.

The same holds a certain water mill; 16s at the said terms.

The same John holds 1 tenement and 30 acres of land in military service from the land formerly of William Bernard; 1 pound of peppers or 12d per annum.

Roger Fyne holds 1 piece of land called Bachilersgroue; ½d per annum. It ought to be allowed [debet allocari] in the rent of William Adam.

John Munde holds 1 messuage there and 30 acres of land by military service; 13d at the said terms. The lady will have wardship, marriage-right, feudal relief and heriot from him when they fall due.

Geoffrey atte Churche holds 1 tenement there and 16 acres of land by military service; 4s 3d per annum at the said terms. He does suit of court. The lady will have wardship, marriage-right and heriot when they fall due.

William atte Doune holds half an acre of land in military service; 6d per annum at the said terms. He does suit of court twice in the year for all except royal service [pro omni seruicio saluo regali].

Luke le Tayllour holds 2 acres of land by military service; 8d per annum at the said terms.

Gilbert atte Wode holds in Litele Brumlegh 20 acres of land by military service; 4s 4d per annum at the said terms. Suit of court. The lady will have wardship, marriage-right, feudal relief and heriot when they fall due.

Christine la Dyghe and Thomas her son hold 1 piece of land called Dyghescrofte in military service; 2s 10d per annum. Wardship, marriage-right and heriot when they fall due.

---

[6] This repetition is as written in the manuscript.

Agnes la Mulnere holds land there that Geoffrey Newman sometime held; 5s per annum at the said terms. She does suit of court. The lady will have wardship, marriage-right, feudal relief and heriot when they fall due.

Adam de La Ryuer holds at will of the lady a certain plot called La Ryuerponde; 12d per annum.

The same Adam holds La Ryuerlonde in military service by hereditary succession from Eustace, his father, which particular land Arnold Piscator [*the fisherman*] once held; 3s per annum at the said terms. Suit of court. The lady will have wardship, marriage-right and heriot when they fall due.

John Herdekyn and Juliana his wife hold by military service the land called Cokemannislond; 18d per annum at the said terms. He does suit of court. The lady will have wardship, marriage-right, heriot etc. [*sic*] when they fall due.

Bartholomew Le Tayllour holds 4 acres of land by military service; 19d per annum. The lady will have wardship, marriage-right, heriot etc. when they fall due.

Thomas Le Somenour holds 1½ acres 1 rod in Odelondefelde; 2d per annum.

William Somenour holds 1½ acres 1 rod; 2d per annum.

Christine Dyghe holds ½ acre 1 rod; 2d per annum.

Mabel Batyn holds ½ acre 1 rod; [no amount of rent given].

Sarah Stanpard holds 1 perch there; [no amount of rent given].

Roger Fyne holds ½ acre 1 rod of land; 2d per annum.

Katherine atte Mersche[7] holds, by name of wardship that she obtains from the lady by fine, 1 messuage and 12 acres of land; [blank] per annum at the four terms. Suit of court every third week. Wardship, marriage-right, feudal relief and heriot when they fall due.

Robert atte Fryth holds 1 tenement and [blank] acres of land; [blank] at the four terms. He does suit of court. Wardship, marriage-right, feudal relief and heriot when they fall due.

William Cok holds 1 tenement and [blank] acres of land; [blank] per annum at the four terms. He does suit of court. The lady will have wardship, marriage-right, feudal relief and heriot when they fall due.
Sum total rent of the free tenants 72s 1½d.

---

[7] The word Hardelegh is written in the left margin next to Katherine's name. Her name is the first of three underlined in this transcription. In the manuscript, they are shown as owing 4s rent in total.

[Bonded tenants]

John Borgh, free in body, holds in bondage at Sheddon 1 tenement and 10 acres of land; 12*d* per annum at the said terms.

> In his working year when it comes round he must carry out 24 works from the feast of Saint Michael until Easter. The work is worth 1*d*.

> And if he will do threshing as the work then 4 bushels of rye or 4 bushels of barley or 10 bushels of oats count as 1 work.

> And in the year that he works he will have allowance of 6*d* of his rent. These works are worth 2*s*. And he will do these aforesaid works every third year.

> And once he has done these works in his year he will be quit of these works for the two following years.

> And he must hoe in every year for 3 half days with 1 man. For that he will have ½*d* on the third day. This work is worth 1*d*.

> And he must do hay-making for the lady for half a day with one man or he will give ½*d*. And thus the work is worth ½*d*.

> And he must reap on every working day in the Autumn with 1 man while the corn of the lady needs reaping. And he will have a meal twice in the day and 1 loaf of bread for dinner, or he will give 14*d* instead of the reaping, and this is anciently determined to be better on account of the great cost of lunch. And thus this work is worth 14*d*.

> And he must shear 5 sheep without food and the work is worth ¼*d*.

> And in every year he will, on the feast of the Nativity of the Lord, give 1 hen, and on the feast of Easter 2½ eggs. The hen is worth 2*d* and the eggs ¾*d*.

> And thus his services in every year are worth 2*s* 1⅞*d*.

> And he will be the reeve if elected and then he will be quit of all his aforementioned rent and services.

> And he may not educate his son nor allow his daughter to marry without permission of the lady.

Geoffrey Bymylaz, villein, holds 1 tenement and 10 acres of land in bondage; 12*d* per annum at the said terms. And he will do all the same services and in the same manner as the said John. He will gain as the said John in every way. And his services, uncertain as above, are worth 2*s* 1⅞*d*.

Geoffrey the reeve, villein, holds 1 tenement and 24 acres of land in bondage; 3*s* 6*d* per annum at the said terms. And he will duplicate the services of the aforementioned John in every way. And in addition to that he will help with the hay-making for the lady for 1 day beyond the duplication of the work in the meadow of the said John. And he will give 5 eggs, again more than duplicating that of the said John. And thus his works are worth in each year 4*s* 4½*d*. And each of the said bondsmen, he will give his best beast for heriot when he dies. And if the aforementioned Geoffrey will be reeve then he will be quit of all his aforesaid rent and services.

The sum of rents of the aforesaid bondsmen 5s 6d.

*The sum of the value of the services of them per annum with the rent, hens and eggs,
8s 8¼d.*

The sum of 4 hens and 15 eggs as rent per annum.

[*Decay of rent*][8]

There are in that place in decay of rent those following as a burden of the accounts
from year to year. Namely:

Of Robert atte Fen, 2*s* 4*d*, per annum because that tenement is in the demesne of
the lady.
The rent of the land of Manston, 2*d*, because the land is in the hand of the lady and
has been let out to farm.
The rent of the tenement of Matilda atte Weststrete, 2*s;* it is a tenement in the
demesne of the lady.
The rent of John Schypman, 4*d;* it is a tenement in the hand of the lady, namely the
Pond.
The rent of Ralph Somenur, 3*s* 6*d;* it is a tenement in the demesne of the lady.
The rent of Eustace atte Slo, 8*d*.
The rent of Jowett [*Iouwete*] atte Byrchete, 12*d*, because nobody knows the land and
its service [*feodum*].
The rent of Walter Cissor per annum 20*d* because the tenement is in the hand of the
lady, namely Pond Caperoun,[9] and it is not found in this new extent.

The sum of the aforesaid rent in decay 13s 6d.

[*Defect of works*]

For defect of works of the said tenants the following are in debit and in allowance:
Matilda atte Weststrete, 2*s* 4*d*, and for defect of works Eustace atte Slo, 14*d*.

The sum of the decay of works 3s 6d

[*Decay of hens*]

In decay Matilda Weststrete, Eustace atte Slo and Eustace Campioun for 3 hens
per annum.

[*Items at farm*]
Robert le Porter holds 2 acres in Coluercroft and the rushes in the marsh of the lady
for the term of his life; 6*d* per annum by charter.

---

8   'Decay' meaning reduced or lost.
9   The surname Caperoun or Caproun is seen elsewhere in Essex; see Jennifer C. Ward
and Essex Record Office, *The Medieval Essex Community: The Lay Subsidy of 1327*, Essex
Historical Documents, 1 (Essex Record Office, 1983), p. 13.

Nicholas de Welyngton holds Manstonelonde; 7*s* per annum to the lady, and 12*s* to Robert le Porter but it is not known by what warrant.

The farm of the dovecot 2*s* per annum handed over to Nicholas de Welyngton.

From the heirs of William Batyn 2*s* for an unknown pasture.

The sum of the farms 11s 6s.

The sum total of all rents of the free and bonded tenants with their services £4 17s 9¾d.

Note that the measurement of the land under meadow and of woodland for the same manor is written down after the extent of Gusford.[10]

[*The demesne*]

The measurement of the lands, woodlands, meadows and pasture that are in the demesne of the manor of Sheddon, made in the month of September, in the fourth year of the blessing of lady Margaret [Aunger], by the grace of God, Abbess of Leigh.[11]

A curtilage with garden there contains 10 acres and 12 perches; value 10*s* per annum.
A wood above the curtilage garden towards the south and towards the chapel contains 37½ acres 1 rod 39 perches and is worth 114*s*, by the acre 3*s*.
There is a small croft of arable land in the same wood that contains 2 acres 20 perches.
The small croft next to Dufhuffeld contains 1 acre 30 perches.
Dufhuffeld contains 3½ acres 5½ perches.
Robert le Porter holds 2 acres for his lifetime from the lady in the same field.
Merthfeld contains 29 acres 11 perches of arable land.
Henftekenslonde contains 74½ acres 1 rod 9½ perches.
Somenoreslonde contains 8 ½ acres 1 rod 37 perches of arable land [fallow].
There is in the same field a piece of land that is laid to meadow because it is being improved that contains 1 rod 32 perches.
Holcroft contains 15 ½ acres 5 perches [fallow].
Litelhocroft contains 4 acres 33 ¼ perches [fallow].
Pyrifeld contains 3½ acres 24½ perches [fallow].
Brodefeld contains 9 acres 29 perches.
Deneuoteslond contains 4½ acres 4½ perches.
Dyndmullefeld contains 15½ acres 1 rod 31½ perches.
Berland contains 11½ acres 12½ perches.
Campiounesdoune contains 5 acres 1 rod 23 perches.
Goulelond contains 13½ acres 28½ perches.
Campiounespytzel contains 1½ acres 33 perches.

[10]   At this point, the manuscript entry for Sheddon jumps from fol. 153v to fol. 162v.
[11]   September 1323.

The sum of the acres of arable land 255½ acres. The value of the extent as above £8 10s 4d, namely 8d per acre.

[*Meadow*]

Mershmede contains 9 acres 3½ perches.
Moltesmede contains 1 rod 17½ perches.
A certain piece of land in Somenoreslond is laid to meadow because that is being improved and contains 1 rod 32 perches.

Sum of the acres of meadow 9 ½ acres 1 rod 13 perches.
Value 39s, namely 4s per acre.

[*Pasture*]

In Langefen are 2 pieces of pasture containing 2 acres 7½ perches.
Fenlond contains 2 acres 23½ perches of pasture.
In Goulefen is a piece of pasture that contains ½ acre 32½ perches.
Benardespytzel contains ½ acre 25 perches of pasture.

Sum of the acres of pasture 5½ acres 8½ perches.
Value 3s 8d, namely 8d per acre.

[*Alder wood*]

Goulefen contains 5½ acres 11½ perches of alder.
Campiounsfen contains 8½ acres 1 rod 21 perches of alder.
A piece of fen next to Brodefeld contains ½ acre 1 rod 24 perches of alder.
Moltefen contains ½ acre 1 rod 6½ perches of alder.
Langefen contains 15 acres 34 perches of alder.

Sum of acres of alder wood 31 acres 1 rod 17 perches.
Value £4 13s 9d, namely 3s per acre.

Sum total value of the demesne by the extent as let through £15 6s 9d.

The sum of the rents and services of that very manor £4 17s 9¾d.

The sum value of the perquisites of the court and the customs of the market £4 6s 8d.

Sum of the farmers with the farm in Manningtree 17s 9d.

The sum of the entire extent let through with Manningtree £28 19s 4½d

Note there are in the demesne of the aforesaid manor at Manstonelond 10 acres that are worth per annum 6s 8d, price 8d per acre as above. The marsh by the sea contains 3 acres, price 8d per acre.

There is there a certain place in which was formerly sited a windmill that used to pay at farm 2 marks and is now consumed with age; the timber from there is sold but the ironwork remains and 2 broken millstones with the pieces of them useless.

Note there are in that place two fish-ponds that contain by estimation 4 acres. They are not given a valuation because no profit proceeds from there.

Town of Manningtree

[*Manitre*]

The extent, rental and custumal made in that place on Tuesday on the vigil of Saint Lawrence the Martyr in the seventeenth year of the reign of King Edward son of King Edward, the third year of Lady Margaret [Aunger] as abbess, by all the homage of that place.[1]

[*Tenants*]

William Wellere, Adam Sextayn and Agnes Mulner hold in Cornhillestrete 1 tenement that was sometime Katherine Slyp's; 6*d* per annum at the four terms; also a halfpenny at Easter and on the feast of St Michael. Feudal relief when it falls due.[2]

Thomas le Gros holds in that same place 1 tenement that was Robert de Mystelegh's; 13*d* at the four terms. Feudal relief when it falls due.

The same Thomas holds 1 tenement that was Agnes Aunsel's; 1½*d* per annum for all service except feudal relief.

John Herdekyn and Juliana his wife hold 1 tenement that was sometime Adam le Cran's; 8*d* at the aforesaid terms. And he does suit of court from that place. Feudal relief when it falls due.

John de Glemmesforde holds there 1 tenement that was Robert le Porter's; 15*d* per annum. Feudal relief when it falls due.

Walter Prustessone holds there 1 tenement in Tynkere Place; 6*d* per annum. Feudal relief when it falls due.

Robert Clerk holds 1 tenement in the same place; 6*d* per annum at the four terms; suit of court. Feudal relief when it falls due.

The same Robert holds 1 tenement next to the tenement of John de Glemmesforde.[3]

Luke le Tayllour holds 1 tenement next to la Tolhouse; 9*d* per annum at the four terms. Feudal relief when it falls due.

---

[1] On Tuesday, 9 August 1323. The term 'all the homage' probably refers to the tenantry of the town; there is no separate list of jurors.
[2] *Cornhilestrete* is written in the left-hand margin besides this entry.
[3] The word *inquiratur* (it should be examined) is written in the left-hand margin beside this entry.

Alex' Waryn holds 1 plot of land there; 3*d* at the aforementioned terms. Feudal relief when it falls due.

William Adam holds 1 plot of land there called Cokeygnesplace; 12*d* at the four terms. Feudal relief when it falls due.

John Bakere and Katherine Frere hold 1 tenement there that was John Carpentar's; 12*d* per annum at the four terms. Feudal relief when it falls due.

Olive de Fynnesforde hold there 1 tenement; 6*d* at the aforementioned terms. Feudal relief when it falls due.

Geoffrey le Jay holds there 1 tenement; 6*d* at the aforementioned terms. Feudal relief when it falls due.

Robert le Smyth holds there 1 tenement; 6*d* at the aforementioned terms. Feudal relief when it falls due.

Thomas le Gros holds there 1 tenement that was John Carpentar's; 16*d* at the aforementioned terms. Feudal relief when it falls due.

Joan Somenur holds there 1 tenement that was formerly Adam Lymhous's; 6*d* at the aforementioned terms. Feudal relief when it falls due.

The same Joan holds 1 tenement called Tolousein, Pleysaunte Lane; 6*d* at the aforementioned terms. Feudal relief when it falls due.

John le Mulner holds 1 tenement in Cornhillestrete; 1½*d* per annum. Feudal relief when it falls due.

The same John holds 1 tenement that was Adam Kelye's; 6*d* per annum at the four terms. Feudal relief when it falls due.

The same John holds a certain house next to his tenement on the west side that was formerly R. Kelia's; 2*d* per annum not obtained that ought to be allocated in the rent of J. Munde [*non sumantur quod debet allocari in redditu .j. munde*].⁴ Feudal relief when it falls due.

Osbert Stonyliuere holds 1 market-stall [*scamellum*] there; 6*d* per annum. Feudal relief when it falls due.

Roger Fyne holds there 1 tenement that was Henry Ganger's; 6*d* at the aforementioned terms. Feudal relief when it falls due.

---

4   This is probably the Johanna (*Joan*) Munde listed on fol. 155r. The meaning may be that 2*d* should be added to what Joan should pay as there is nothing forthcoming from John le Mulner.

Roger Teselere holds there half of a shop [*dimidiam Schoppam*]; 2*d* per annum. Feudal relief when it falls due.

Isabel Chepman holds there the other half of a shop; 2*d* per annum. Feudal relief when it falls due.

John Dale holds there 1 shop; 4*d* per annum. Feudal relief when it falls due.

The wife of John de Allesford holds there 1 shop; 4*d* per annum. Feudal relief when it falls due.

Roger atte Stronde holds there 1 tenement that was formerly Puttehund's; 2*s* 2*d* at the aforementioned terms. Feudal relief when it falls due.

The same Roger holds 1 shop that is from the same house [*de eadem domo*].[5]

John Gernoun holds there 1 tenement; 2*s* 8½*d* per annum; he does suit of court. Feudal relief when it falls due.

Luke le Tayllour holds in Chapellestrete 1 shop and 1 market-stall; 2½*d* per annum. Feudal relief when it falls due.

Isabel Gernoun holds there 1 shop from Joan Munde. In what manner is to be inquired and the charter is to be seen.[6]

Roger Fyne holds 1 tenement in Pleysauntelane; 20*d* per annum at the four terms. Feudal relief when it falls due.

The same Roger holds there 1 tenement that was Adam Lymhous's; 6*d* at the four terms. Feudal relief when it falls due.

The same Roger holds there 1 tenement that was Walter Boltere's; 6*d* at the aforementioned terms. Feudal relief when it falls due.

William Kebbel holds there 1 tenement from Joan Gernoun. In what manner is to be inquired and the charter is to be seen.[7]

Thomas Alfeld holds there 1 tenement from Joan Munde. In what manner is to be inquired and the charter is to be seen.[8]

Alfelda the wife of Adam Le Reue holds 1 tenement there from Joan Munde. In what manner is to be inquired and the charter is to be seen.[9]

---

[5] A note in the right-hand margin links the two entries for Roger atte Stronde to say *2s 2d in toto*.

[6] There is note in the left-hand margin next to this entry that says *to be inquired* (*inquiratur*).

[7] Another *inquiratur*.

[8] *Inquiratur*.

[9] *Inquiratur*.

Roger Fyne holds there 1 tenement to the north side of the Chapel [*in parte Boriali Capelle*] that was Smallham's; 3s 6d at the aforementioned terms. Feudal relief when it falls due.

The same Roger holds 1 tenement to the south side of the Chapel [*in parte Australi Capelle*] that was Nicholas Gernoun's; 3s at the aforementioned terms. Feudal relief when it falls due.

John Druer and Roger Fyne hold a piece of land with 1 ditch containing a water-course [*fundum .j. fossatum cum cursu aque in eodem*] next to their messuage; 1d per annum for all service.

Robert Stace holds 1 tenement there that was Simon Godale's; 1 pound of wax to the Chapel per annum. The charter is to be seen if that is the case.[10]

The same Robert holds 1 plot that was Sarkyn's; 1 pound of wax to the Chapel per annum. The charter is to be seen if that is the case.

The same Robert holds 1 tenement in Southetoune; 2d at the aforementioned terms. Feudal relief when it falls due.

Joan Flourette de Bereholte holds 1 shop and a curtilage there; 1d at Easter and at the feast of St Michael because it should be allocated in the rent of R. Buxton.

Richard Buxton holds 1 tenement there; nothing is due as Robert Stace makes payment to the Chapel for everything.[11]

The same Richard holds 1 tenement there that was Richard Le Hy's; 8d at the afore-mentioned terms. Feudal relief when it falls due.

Hubert Lehurde holds 1 tenement there; 1 pound of wax to the Chapel per annum.[12]

Richard Lehurde holds 1 tenement there; 3d at the aforementioned terms. Feudal relief when it falls due.

William Somenur holds 1 tenement there; 3d at the aforementioned terms. Feudal relief when it falls due.

John Dygelegh holds 1 tenement there; 9d at the aforementioned terms. Feudal relief when it falls due.

Roger Pacche holds 1 unbuilt [*non edificatam*] plot there; 3d at the aforementioned terms. Feudal relief when it falls due.

---

[10] *Inquiratur.*
[11] *Inquiratur.*
[12] *Inquiratur.*

Mabel Batyn holds 1 tenement there; 9*d* at the aforementioned terms. Feudal relief when it falls due.

Robert Munt holds 1 tenement there; 6*d* at the aforementioned terms. Feudal relief when it falls due. Two suits of court at the feasts of Easter and St Michael.

Walter Tayllour holds there 1 tenement; 6*d* at the aforementioned terms. Feudal relief when it falls due.[13]

John Borgh holds 1 tenement there; 6*d* at the aforementioned terms. Feudal relief when it falls due.

Bartholomew Coupere holds 1 tenement there; 4*d* per annum. Feudal relief when it falls due.

Richard Buxton holds 1 plot that was Simon Sutor's; 6*d* at the aforementioned terms. Feudal relief when it falls due.

The same Richard holds 1 plot there that belonged to the son of the reeve; 6*d* at the aforementioned terms. Feudal relief when it falls due.

Agnes Somenour holds 1 tenement there; 2*d* per annum from the tenement of Thomas Clerk. Feudal relief when it falls due.

Thomas Somenour holds 1 tenement there; 2*d* per annum according to the same [*de eodem*]. Feudal relief when it falls due.

William Somenour holds 1 tenement from the same tenement there; 2*d* per annum. Feudal relief when it falls due.

Sarah Stanpard holds 1 tenement there; 6*d* at the aforementioned terms. Also 2*d* for a quarter part of the tenement that was Thomas Clerk's. Feudal relief when it falls due.

John Somenour holds 1 tenement there; 8*d* at the aforementioned terms. Feudal relief when it falls due.

Christine La Dyghe holds 1 tenement in Pernelelane that was Thomas Alfeld's; 6*d* at the aforementioned terms. Feudal relief when it falls due.

Lord Richard de Castreton, lord of Lalleford, holds 1 tenement there; 18*d* at the aforementioned terms. Feudal relief when it falls due.[14]

---

[13] There is a marginal note linking this entry to the next one (John Borgh). It says to enquire whether these two should pay 12*d* or 6*d*?

[14] The Casterton referred to here is probably either Great Casterton or Little Casterton in Rutland (both to the north-west of Stamford). The name Richard de Casterton is mentioned in records for that area (see https://www.british-history.ac.uk/vch/rutland/vol2/pp232-236 [accessed 30 Jan. 2025]). There is a Lalleford Manor in Bedfordshire, although any records for there survive from no earlier than 1425 (see https://bedsarchives.bedford.gov.uk/

Robert Le Smyth holds 1 tenement there from the tenement of Thomas Cnop; 3*d* at the aforementioned terms. Feudal relief when it falls due.

Robert Wyslade holds 1 tenement there; 3*d* at the aforementioned terms. Feudal relief when it falls due.

Christine Dighe holds 1 plot that was Buschmanesplace; 6*d* at the aforementioned terms. Feudal relief when it falls due.

Robert Munt holds the tenement La Werkhous there; 6*d* at the aforementioned terms. Feudal relief when it falls due.

The same Robert holds 1 plot of length 10 virgates and width 6 virgates next to La Ponde; 2*d* per annum.[15]

Joan Caperoun holds 1 tenement; 2*s* per annum at the four terms. Feudal relief when it falls due.

Alice Gernoun holds 1 tenement there; 12*d* at the four terms. She must do suit of court. Feudal relief when it falls due.

Pety Water holds 1 tenement there from William Frank.[16]

Reginald Mazoun holds 1 tenement there; 8*d* at the aforementioned terms. Feudal relief when it falls due.

William Le Reue holds 1 tenement there; 12*d* per annum to the Chapel, the charter is to be seen.[17]

John Sankyn holds 1 tenement there; 2*d* at the aforementioned terms. Feudal relief when it falls due.

John Le Dryuere holds 1 tenement there; ¼*d* per annum. Feudal relief when it falls due.

Richard Buxton and Mabel Batyn hold 1 tenement; ¼*d* per annum. Feudal relief when it falls due.

Reginald Le Mazoun holds 1 shop there that was Christina Horkeslegh's; 1*d* per annum. Feudal relief when it falls due.

CommunityHistories/Luton/LutonIntroduction/LalllefordManorLuton.aspx [accessed 30 Jan. 2025]).

[15] In this context, the term virgate (*virgarum*) probably mean yards, although it could also mean rods. The virgate of 20 or 30 acres seems very unlikely.

[16] *Inquiratur.*

[17] *Inquiratur.*

Adam atte Lymhous holds 1 tenement there from Joan Munde, the charter is to be seen.[18]

Roger atte Stronde holds 1 tenement there that was Bartholomew Le Tayllour's; *6d* at the aforementioned terms. Feudal relief when it falls due.

Walter Le Reue holds 1 tenement there; *8d* per annum at the aforementioned terms. Feudal relief when it falls due.

Luke Le Tayllour holds 1 tenement there that was Hubert de Doune's; *3s 6d* per annum at the said four terms. He does suit of court. Feudal relief when it falls due.

Agnes Louekyn holds 1 tenement there; *4d* per annum at the four terms. Feudal relief when it falls due.

Nicholas Louekyn holds 1 tenement there; *8d* at the four terms. Suit of court. Feudal relief when it falls due.

Lord John le Dyghe holds there 1 tenement; *12d* at the aforementioned terms. Suit of court. Feudal relief when it falls due.

Walter Tayllour holds 1 tenement there; *12d* at the four terms. He does suit of court. Feudal relief when it falls due.

Roger atte Stronde holds there 1 tenement that was Stephen Betoun's; *9d* per annum. Feudal relief when it falls due.

Bartholomew Le Tayllour holds 1 tenement there that was William Riper's; *6d* per annum. Feudal relief when it falls due.

Christine Dyghe holds 1 tenement there that was Nicholas Gernoun's; *4d* per annum. Feudal relief when it falls due.

Thomas Dyghe holds 1 tenement there; *8d* at the aforementioned terms. Feudal relief when it falls due.

Christine Dyghe holds 1 tenement there from Christine Louekyn, in what manner is to be seen.[19]

Christine Louekyn holds 1 tenement there that was Henry Caperoun's; *6d* per annum. Feudal relief when it falls due.

Henry Caperoun holds 1 tenement there from the lady abbess that is part of the tenement of Christine Louekyn; payment to Lord John de Brokenurth *12d* of

---

[18] *Inquiratur.*
[19] *Inquiratur.*

rent-seck [*de sicco redditu*], to the abbess nil, because the said Christine bears a charge [*portet*] of 6*d* for both tenements.[20]

Nicholas de Welyngton holds 1 tenement there; 9*d* at the aforementioned terms; also 1½*d* for Caye. Suit of court. Feudal relief when it falls due.

The same Nicholas and Henry Caperoun, shared between them [*diuisum inter eos*], hold 1 tenement that was the bake-house [*pistrina*] of Henry Caperoun; 6*d* per annum. Feudal relief when it falls due.

Thomas Le Smyth holds 1 tenement from Walter atte Wylle of Colchester. In what manner he holds is to be seen.

John Herkyn holds 1 tenement from Joan Munde; he must do suit of court. In what manner he holds is to be seen.

John Le Mulner and Christine his wife hold 1 tenement that was once Simon de Spina's; 12*d* per annum. Feudal relief when it falls due.

Robert Lomunt holds 1 tenement that was Robert Perdrych's; 12*s* per annum. Feudal relief when it falls due.

Christine Fyne holds 1 tenement there; 8*d* at the aforementioned terms. Feudal relief when it falls due.

John Somenour holds 1 tenement there; 14*d* at the four terms. Feudal relief when it falls due.

John Frank holds 1 tenement there from William Adam. It is to be seen in what manner.

Adam atte Ryvere holds 1 tenement; 12*d* per annum. Feudal relief when it falls due.

Walter Le Somenour holds 1 tenement there; 12*d* per annum. He does two suits of court for a reasonable sum [*per rationabilem summam*]. Feudal relief when it falls due.

William Adam holds his 1 tenement in Manitree from the heirs of Robert Adam for the service of 1 clove of garlic [*.j. cloui gariofili*] per annum.

Lord John de Cottone, rector of the church of Wrabness [*Wrabbenose*] holds there 1 tenement; 4*d* per annum. Feudal relief when it falls due.[21]

---

[20] *Redditus siccus* is rent-seck (without power of distress) – see Latham, *Revised Medieval Word-List*, p. 396. It is a rent granted to a person other than the owner of the income property, without right of distress for non-payment. Another *inquiratur*.
[21] The Church of All Saints, Wrabness, was in the patronage of the Abbey of Bury. Sir John de Cottone was already rector there in 1308 (https://archive.org/stream/threeroydonfamilooroyd/threeroydonfamilooroyd_djvu.txt [accessed 3 Oct. 2024], quoting Harleian Charter 55, c.27).

Walter Daubere holds 1 tenement there; 4*d* per annum. Feudal relief when it falls due.

John Fyne holds 1 tenement there; 8*d* at the four terms. Feudal relief when it falls due.

Luke Le Tayllour holds 1 tenement there that was Christine ni [*sic*] Fraunk's; 8*d* per annum. Feudal relief when it falls due.[22]

John Munde holds 1 tenement there; 1*s* per annum. Suit of court. And feudal relief from which John Mulner will acquit himself of 2*d* from the tenement that was Robert Kelye's.

William Herkestyde holds 1 tenement there from J. Mund, in what manner is to be seen.[23]

Henry Caperoun holds 1 plot of Caye; 1½*d* per annum. And feudal due.

John Le Tayllour holds 1 plot of Caye there; 1½*d* per annum; And feudal relief etc. [*sic*].

Agnes Louekyn holds 1 plot of land there that Robert Attstone held by concession of abbess Matilda; 2*d* per annum at the four terms.[24]

Walter Sumenour holds 1 plot next to the salt water [*iuxta aquam salsam*] that Walter Jay sometime held; 2*d* per annum.

John Le Tayllour and Juliana his wife hold 1 plot next to the marsh [*iuxta mariscum*]; 2*d* per annum. Feudal relief when it falls due.

Roger atte Stronde holds 1 market-stall; 1*d* per annum.

John Herkyn holds 1 market-stall.[25]

Walter le Reue holds 1 market-stall relating to a tenement; nil owing.[26]

William Herkestede holds 1 tenement; 12¾*d* per annum. Feudal relief when it falls due.

Sum Total of the Rents of Manningtree per annum 70s 4¾d.

[*Items held at farm*]
Robert Le Smyth holds the forge next to La Tolhouse at farm; 2*s* 6*d* per annum at the four terms for all services.

---

[22] It may be that the use of *ni* here is equivalent to née.
[23] Another *inquiratur*.
[24] Matilda la Tablere was abbess from October 1284 until October 1306.
[25] *Inquiratur*.
[26] *Inquiratur*.

John le Ryche holds 1 house next to John Gernoun at farm; 2*s* at the aforementioned terms for all services.

Ralph Quist holds 1 market-stall at farm; 12*d* per annum at the aforementioned terms for all services.

Adam Dygoun for 1 market-stall next to the tenement of J. Mulnere; 4*d* per annum for all services.

Robert Souter for 1 market-stall there; 3*d* per annum for all services.

[name left blank] for 1 market-stall there; 3*d* per annum for all services.

Sum of all the farms there 6s 3d.

Manor of Gusford

[*Guthelesford*]

Extent, rental and custumal made there on Thursday next after the feast of Saint Laurence the Martyr in the seventeenth year of the reign of King Edward son of King Edward [4 August 1323], the third year of lady Margaret [Aunger] as abbess by full homage of the jurors of the manor who say that:

The Close of the Court [*Clausum Curie*]

The close of the court contains 3½ acres 1 rod 23 perches by measure. The pasture with the bracken growing there is worth 2s per annum, and the fruit of the trees 18d.

In Stancrofte are 3 acres 1 rod 5 perches, value of the acre per annum 3d
In Thursmede WenWente are 2 acres 8 perches, value per acre 3d per annum
In Dungatewente are 4 acres 20 perches, value per acre 3d per annum
In PorteWeyeWente are 3 acres 1 rod 24 perches, value per acre 3d per annum
In Wodesrethe are 7 acres 1 rod, value per acre 3½d per annum
In Leghes are 5½ acres 1 rod 20 perches, value per acre 3d per annum
In Banelonde are 8 acres and in Mulnefelde 4½ acres, value per acre 3½d per annum
Beneath the wood of Saltemedewe are 3 acres 1 rod 26 perches, value per acre 3d per annum
In Mulneresacre 1 acre 1 rod 30 perches, value per acre 3½d per annum
In Chalkyacre is 1 acre, value per acre 3d per annum
In Stokhillonde are 3½ acres, value per acre 3d per annum
In a piece of land at Seyteresbus are 2 acres 30 perches, value per acre 3d per annum
In la Breggelonde are 8½ acres, value per acre 3d per annum
In a piece of land situated between Clyfwalle and Seyterebus 6½ acres 1 rod, value per acre 3½d per annum

The sum of the acreages of arable land 65 acres 1 rod 3 perches
Value from the above extent 17s 5¾d

Meadows

In Brademedwene are 2 acres, value 4s per annum
At the Cross ½ acre, value 2s per annum
At Countesfordemedwene 1 acre, value 18d per annum
In La Dammemedwene 2 acre 10 perches, value 4s 1½d per annum
In Myddelmedwene 3 rods, value 10d per annum
At Leghes 1 acre 1 rod 15 perches, value 18d per annum
In Thursmedwene 1½ acres, value 18d per annum
In La Callemersch 1 acre 1 rod, value 10d per annum

The sum of the acreages of meadow with Callemersch 10 acres 1 rod 25 perches
Value from the above extent 16s 3½d

Woods

There are by measure 14 acres of coppice-wood there to be cut down [*prosterni*] every five years and not to be left standing for further benefit [*et non ulterius stare ad commodum*]. And then the crop of them [*vestura eiusdem*] is worth 30s in an average year [*communibus annis*]. And thus each portion of them for sale annually is worth 6s.

Sum of the acreages of woodland 14 ½ acres
Value annually from the extent above 6s

The total value of the demesne land with the close of the court, arable land, meadow and woodland from the above extent 43s 3¼d

The Mill

In the same manor there is one water mill that is worth after deductions 40s in an average year

Perquisites of the Court

The perquisites of the manor and leet courts in an average year 20s

Free tenants

Laurence Leffre holds approx. 20 acres of land at Hunchele by military service; 4s at the four terms of the year; 8s as feudal due [*relevium*] when it may fall due

Andrew Arunde holds 1 messuage and approx. 5 acres of land by military service; 2s at the same terms; feudal due and heriot when they may fall due. He will come to the leet court at Gusford held after Michaelmas

The same Andrew holds one piece of land called Mullecrofte; one crown of roses [*.j. coronam de rosis*] on the feast of Saint John the Baptist for all service

William Huberd at La Kalles holds 3 rods of land; 3d at the four terms; he will do suit of court every third week at the court of the lady; he will render feudal due when it should fall due

John Douelers holds 3 rods of land; 3d at the same terms; he owes suit of court just as the said William; he will render feudal due when it should fall due

Robert Aunsel holds 1 messuage and 1 acre of land in Gusford; 12d per annum at the same term for all service except feudal due which he will render when it falls due

William Seman holds 1 tenement in Gusford and 4 acres of land; 21*d* per annum for all service except feudal due when it falls due

Robert Scot holds 1 cottage there and 1 acre of land; 14*d* per annum at the afore-mentioned terms. And he does suit of court and he will render feudal due and heriot when they fall due[1]

Robert le Mulner holds 1 messuage and 2 acres of land; 2*s* 6*d* per annum at the aforementioned terms; he does suit of court; he will render feudal due and heriot when they fall due

Peter Seman holds 1 messuage and 2 acres 3 rods of land; 2*s* 3*d* per annum; and he will render feudal due and heriot when they fall due

Robert Tudery holds 1 house and 1 rod of land; 4*d* per annum; and suit of court, and feudal due and heriot when they fall due

Simon Cok holds 1 house and half a rod of land; 2*d* per annum; he owes feudal due and he will come to the leet court

Thomas Tedery holds 1 house and half a rod of land; 2*d* per annum and feudal due when it falls due; and he will come to the leet court

Adam atte Fenne holds 1 messuage and 7 acres of land; 3*s* 8*d* per annum; he does suit of court; he will render feudal due and heriot when they fall due

Richard Russel through Roysa his wife holds 1 messuage and 6 acres of land; 2*s* 4*d* per annum; he does suit of court; he will render feudal due and heriot when they fall due

William Persoun holds 15 acres of heath land; 5*s* per annum at the four terms; he does suit of court; he will render feudal due when it falls due

Roger Muchelfire holds 1 messuage and 5 acres of land; 12*d* per annum; he does suit of court; he will render feudal due and heriot when they fall due

John Petyt holds 1 house and 1 acre of land, owing per annum [*the first of the three tenants who jointly owe 12d in rent according to a note in the right-hand margin*]

Walter Petyt 1 acre of land [*the second of the three tenants*]

Simon Cok holds 1 house and 1 acre of land, owing per annum [*the third of the three tenants*]

Wymarca Petyt holds 1 cottage for the term of her life; 9*d* per annum at the same terms

---

[1] *Cartulary*, 236, dated April 1309, describes a grant of land to Robert Scot and his wife, Amicia, of half an acre of land together with a house situated between the land of William Seman on one side and John Watte on the other.

The prior of Ipswich holds the land of Douninggeslonde until Alice, the heir of that tenement, comes of age;[2] 3s per annum plus 3s of additional rent [de incremento redditu] until the heir achieves legal majority; the heir, when they achieve legal majority, ought to do suit of court and feudal due and heriot when they fall due

Constance la White holds 4 acres of land by hereditary right; 4d per annum; she will render feudal due when it falls due

Joan Seman holds at will 1 house and 4 acres of land without a deed owing a fine of 12d per annum; and feudal due and heriot when they fall due

The prior of Ipswich holds half an acre of land; 1d at the feast of St Michael and at Easter for all services

The total value of the rents of the aforementioned free tenants 34s

Also 3s of additional rent until the legal majority of Alice, heir of Donnynggeslond

Tenants in Bondage and of Villein Status

In the same manor there are tenants in bondage and of villein status listed below, namely:

Semmanus Gosce holds 1 messuage and 5 acres of land; 8d per annum at the four terms; 1d for maltsilver.[3]

> He will plough 7½ acres between the feast of St Michael and Easter for no payment; the work is worth 2s 2¼d, value per acre 3½d

> He will hoe for 8 half-days with 1 man; the work is worth 4d to the lady

> He will mow for 8 days with 1 man; the work is worth 8d to the lady

> He must reap for each day in the autumn with 1 man and each will do the whole of the lady's corn harvest ; he will have lunch and the value of the autumn work is 14d

> He will help with the carriage of the millstone with one man; and every second year he will give a hen, and every second year 5 eggs; this service is worth 1⅛d

> He must do carriage-service to Manningtree [apud Manitre] and to the nearby markets at the will of the lady; then he will have food; this work has not been given value as it not worth more than the food

> Thus his services are worth 4s 6⅜d

> He will be the reeve if so elected and then he will be quit of his aforementioned rents and services

---

[2] The prior of St Peter's, Ipswich, in 1323 was Henry of Kersey, who had been elected in 1311 (David M. Smith and Vera C. M. London, *The Heads of Religious Houses: England and Wales II, 1216–1377*, The Heads of Religious Houses Series, 1st edn (Cambridge University Press, 2001), p. 396).

[3] Maltsilver is money paid as a tax on the making of malt. The name *Semannus* has no obvious equivalent in modern English.

When he dies he will give heriot of his best beast

He cannot educate his son nor can his daughter marry without permission of the ladies. Nor may any of the tenants written below

Isabel Seman, villein, and Lenota Makel, villein of the lady, hold 1 messuage and 5 acres of land; 8d at the aforementioned terms; 1d for malt silver; they will jointly do all the services as the aforementioned *Semannus*; value 4s 6⅜d; each will render heriot when she dies

Geoffrey Mot and Hamond Douelers, both free in body, hold 1 messuage and 6 acres of land; 3s 4d per annum at the four terms

> They must undertake each week one labour and a half from the feast of St Michael until Easter except for the two weeks of Christmas, value per week 1½d; when threshing is being done they must thresh as their labour 4 bushels of wheat or 4 bushels of rye or 5 bushels of barley or 10 bushels of oats as one labour. They must do this service every third year.

> There are 4 tenants of the same status of whom two of them together must undertake this service in their third year when it falls due.

> The tenant who works the aforementioned service in his year will be quit of the same works for the following two years. And the tenant who in that year works as mentioned above will be quit of 12d from his rent. And this service is worth sometimes more sometimes less according to whether Easter is earlier or is moved later, but on usually 2s, less the 12d of the rent for which he receives the allowance for the work.

> And he must reap just as the aforementioned *Semannus*. Value 14d.

> He will give every year 1 hen and 5 eggs. Value annually 2¼d.

> The value of their works jointly is 3s 4¼d.

> They must do carriage-service as above.

> They will be reeve etc.

> Each will give heriot when he dies.

Alice Orgour, villein, holds 1 messuage and 5 acres of land; 2s per annum at the said terms; she will do each and every service as the aforementioned Geoffrey and Hamond do as stated above that are worth jointly 3s 4¼d per annum

The same Alice holds 1 messuage and 3 acres of land; 20d per annum at the said terms; she must reap in autumn just as the said *Semannus*. The work is worth 14d; no other service is to be done

Thomas Man, free in body, holds 1 messuage and 5 acres of land; 2s per annum at the said terms; he does all the same services as the aforesaid Geoffrey and Hamund; value jointly per annum 3s 4¼d

Alice Seman, villein, holds 1 messuage and 5 acres of land; 2s per annum at the said terms; she does all the same services as the aforementioned Geoffrey and Hamond; value jointly per annum 3s 4¼d

Matilda who was the wife of William Raysoun, free in body, holds 1 messuage and 3 acres of land; 2s per annum at the said terms; she must reap in the autumn just like the said *Semannus*; the work is worth 14d; she will give 2 hens and 5 eggs annually at Christmas; the value is 4¼d

Dulcie atte Crosse, free in body, holds 1 messuage and 2 acres of land; 12d per annum at the said terms; she must reap just as the said *Semannus*; the work is worth 14d; she will give 1 hen and 2½ eggs annually at Christmas; the service is worth 2⅛d

The total rents of the tenants in bondage 17s 4d

The total value of the services of those in bondage with malt silver, hens and eggs 29s 10⅜d

The total number of hens 7 And of eggs 32½

The total value of the entire manor as in the extent as it is let through with the mill and perquisites of the court £9 4s 5½d

Note that the heirs of Peter Anneys should pay by custom 4d per annum for land in Coppedehok, which rent is neglected on account of the suit that was examined for the same tenement for lord Alan de Goldyngham. And they are running in arrears and loss in the account of Gusford.

Note that the heirs of Richard de Holbrok should pay by custom 16d per annum which was let slip in the time of the Countess, and they are running in arrears and loss in the account of Gusford.

Note that the winter works of those who must work at threshing and similar works will be at a fixed rate when Easter happens lower [than] 36 [weeks before Advent Sunday] when such work falls upon one tenant among four [bondmen] who are of the same status. And as Easter is raised [= moved earlier], the works shall be moved [in date?]. And when that allocation of working falls upon two tenants, namely every third year, those works will be doubled according as Easter happens earlier or later. And this custom appears more fully above in the explanation of the works of Geoffrey Mot and Hamond Douelers. Moreover, the other summer and autumn works are placed at a fixed value as is made clear above, namely 16 hoeing [days], value altogether 8d, 16 mowing [days], value 16d. And the reaping of each tenant is placed at a fixed rate for 14d.

Appendix 1. Latin Transcription and English Translation for the Devon Manor of Netherton

.Extent.   .Nytherton.

¶ Extenta manerii de Nytherton' facta ibidem die Lune post festum Nativitatis Sancti Johannis Baptiste, anno domini millesimo .CCCxxiij. et benedictionis Domine Margarete Abbatisse tercio. Per sacramentum Radulphi Dauy,[1] Johannis Matheu, Johannis in the Huyrne, Nicholai Matheu, Henrici Pouke et Thome Clanefeld. Qui dicunt per sacramentum suum quod sunt in eodem manerio de terra arabili in le Estfeld .xlv. acre. Item in Myddelfeld cum Chelfhamcrofte .xliij. acre. Item in Westfeld .xlv. acre.

¶ The extent of the manor of Netherton made in that place on Monday after the feast of the Nativity of St John the Baptist,[2] in the year of the lord 1323 and in the third [year] of the blessing of the lady Margaret, abbess.[3] By the oath of Ralph Davy, John Matheu, John in the Huyrne, Nicholas Matheu, Henry Pouke and Thomas Clanfeld, who say on their oath that in that same manor there are in the Estfeld 45 acres of arable land, also in Myddelfeld with Chelfhamcrofte 43 acres, also in Westfeld 45 acres.

¶ Summa acrarum terre arabilis .Cxxxiij. acre. Et valet acra .iij.d. Et sic in toto .xxxiij.s. .iij.d.

¶ The sum of the acres of arable land is 133 acres. And an acre is worth 3d. And thus in total 33s 3d.

¶ Item sunt ibidem de vasta terra iuxta Cnolhouse .xij. acre. et .vj. acre iuxta Bromlegh'.

¶ Also there are 12 acres of waste land there next to Cnolhouse and 6 acres next to Bromlegh'.

---

[1] There are several instances of Dauy or Davy in *DLS* but no Ralph Dauy.

[2] This feast was celebrated on 24 June. The following Monday in 1323 was on 27 June.

[3] Margaret Aunger had been blessed as abbess on 24 August 1320. She was dead by 8 October 1345 (David M. Smith and Vera C. M. London, *The Heads of Religious Houses: England and Wales, II. 1216–1377*, The Heads of Religious Houses Series, 1st edn (Cambridge University Press, 2001), p. 550, doi:10.1017/CBO9780511495632).

¶ Summa acrarum terre vaste .xviij. acre et valet acra .ij.*d.* et sic in toto .iiij.*s.*

¶ The sum of the acres of waste land is 18 acres and an acre is worth 2*d* and thus in total 3*s.*

¶ Item sunt ibidem de prato videlicet in Pynnoweshele .j. acra, apud Wodham .j. acra, apud Bromleghe .ij. acre dimidia, apud Coweswode .iij. acre, apud Broclond .j. acra, apud Worthy .j. acra, apud Holemede .j. acra .j. pertica, apud la Deremede .ij. acre dimidia .j. pertica, in la Hamme .j. acra dimidia .j. pertica, in Crofte .j. acra dimidia .j. pertica, ~ unde .ij. acre non falcatas nisi secundo anno.

¶ Also there is meadowland there namely in Pynnoweshele 1 acre, at Wodham 1 acre, at Bromleghe 2½ acres, at Coweswode 3 acres, at Broclond 1 acre, at Worthy 1 acre, at Holemede 1 acre & 1 perch, at la Deremede 2½ acres & 1 perch, in la Hamme 1½ acres & 1 perch, in Crofte 1½ acres & 1 perch ~ whereof 2 acres are only mown every other year.

¶ Summa acrarum prati .xvij. acre et valet acra .xij.*d.* preter .ij. acras predictas que non cadunt in extentam que non falcantur. Et sic in toto .xvj.*s.*[4]

¶ The sum of the acres of meadow is 17 acres and an acre is worth 12*d* except for the aforementioned 2 acres that are not mown that do not fall within the extent. And thus in total 16*s.*

¶ Item sunt ibidem de bosco alneto videlicet apud Bromlegh' .iiij. acre. Et in la Hammes .iiij. acre. Et valet acra per annum .iij.*d.*

¶ Also of alder wood there are there namely at Bromlegh 3 acres. And in la Hammes 4 acres. And an acre is worth 3*d* per year.

Summa acrarum prati .vij. acre et valet acra .iij.*d.* Et sic in tot .xxj.*d.*[5]

The sum of the acres of woodland is 7 acres and an acre is worth 3*d.* And thus in total 21*d.*

¶ Item curia cum clauso adiacente .ij. acras. Et valet acra .iij.*d.*

¶ Also the court house with adjoining close [comprises] 2 acres. And an acre is worth 3*d.*

---

[4] The scribe's arithmetic seems a little off. The meadows just mentioned total 16 acres and 4 perches, plus the 2 acres that are described as not mown. However, he then gives as the total 17 acres (a mistake?). He says that the value (at 12*d* or 1*s* per acre) minus 2 acres is 16s. That implies a total of 18 acres, which would make more sense.

[5] This line looks like a scribal error – he surely meant to say *Summa acrarum bosci* etc.

.Nytherton.

¶ Summa .vj.*d.*

¶ Sum 6*d.*

¶ Item sunt super montes que iacent in comuni pastura .lx. acre. Et non extenditur quia iacet in comuni pastura. Nec aliud proficuum capita inde ni- si communis pastura

¶ Also there are 60 acres on the hills that lie as common pasture. And it is not valued because it lies as common pasture. Nor is there another profit in respect of any common pasture.

¶ Item unum columbare ibidem valet per annum .xij.*d.*

¶ Also one dovecot there is worth 12*d* per year.

¶ Item unum molendinum ibidem valet per annum communiter .xxiiij.*s.*

¶ Also a mill there is normally worth 24*s* per year.

¶ Summa valoris terre dominici cum prato, columbari et molendino .Lxxix.*s.* .vj.*d.*

¶ The sum of the value of the demesne land with meadow, the dovecot and mill [is] 79*s* 6*d.*

* Item heredes Jordani de Wyteleghe pro .j. acra dimidia prati in Langemede ob. soluendo ad Pascham.

* Also the heirs of Jordan of Wyteleghe for 1½ acres of meadow in Langemede pay ½*d*, due at Easter.[6]

* Heredes Thome de Bromleghe pro terra de Putteley et Wytheham .ij.*d.* soluendo ad festum Nativitatis Sancti Johannis Baptiste et Sancti Michaelis ex dono Willelmi le Harpur ut patet per cartam suam super numerum .x.

* The heirs of Thomas de Bromleghe for the land of Putteley and Wytheman pay 2*d* owing at the feasts of the Nativity of St John the Baptist and of St Michael from the gift of William le Harpur as is clear in his charter at number X.[7]

---

[6]   Whitley (Witheleghe, Wyteleghe) lay in the parish of Farway (*Cartulary*, p. xxvii).
[7]   See *Cartulary*, item 164 (p. 60). The feast of St Michael the archangel (Michaelmas) is on 29 September.

* Willelmus de Clanefelde tenet .ij. ferlingos terre ibidem ad vitam suam et Johanne uxoris sue per cartam reddendo inde annuatim ad .iiij. terminos .viij.s. .x.d. ob. videlicet ad festa Nativitatis Domini, Pasche et Sancti Michaelis equis porcionibus pro omnibus serviciis preter sectam curie et guldabit in amerciamentis communibus cum bondis.

* William de Clanefelde holds 2 ferlings[8] of land there for the term of his life and the life of Joan his wife by charter whence paying annually at three fixed dates 8s 10½d, namely at the feasts of the Nativity of the Lord, Easter and St Michael in equal portions for all services besides suit of court,[9] and he will pay tax in the usual money payments with the bonded tenants.[10]

* Symon Deueneys tenet .j. ferlingum terre ibidem ad vitam suam reddendo inde per annum .v.s. pro omnibus serviciis preter sectam curie.[11]

* Simon Deveneys holds one ferling of land there for the term of his life for which he pays 5s per year for all services besides suit of court.

* Rogerus Stowey liber tenet in feodo hereditario .j. ferlingum terre et .j. tenementum apud Stoweye reddendo inde per annum ad tres terminos predictos .ij.s. et .vj.d. pro omnibus serviciis preter sectam curie. Et saluo seruicio regali quantum pertinet ad tantum terre.

* Roger Stowey freeman holds one ferling of land and one tenement at Stoweye in hereditary fee for which he pays 2s 6d per year at the three aforementioned terms for all services besides suit of court, and save for service to the king (however much should pertain to land of such size).

* Item Johanna Deueneys tenet .j. ferlingum terre ad vitam suam per cartam reddendo ad terminos predictos .v.s. .iiij.d. Et arabit per .ij. dies de prece si boues habeat cum cibo. Et valet opus .vj.d. Item debet metere per .iiij. dies cum .j. homine de prece et habere prandium et valet opus Domine .v.d. Item debet iuuare ad mullonem feni et valet opus ob.

* Also Joan Deveneys holds by charter one ferling of land for the term of her life paying at the aforementioned terms 5s 3d. And if she has the oxen she will plough with food for 2 days as boon work.[12] And the work is worth 6d. Also she must reap with one man for 4 days as boon work and to have dinner, and the work is worth 6d to the Lady. Also she must help with the stacking of the hay and the work is worth ½d.

---

[8] A ferling is usually (though not always) defined as a quarter of a virgate. The definition of a virgate can also vary but is often given as 30 acres (P. D. A. Harvey, *Manorial Records, Archives and the User*, 5, rev. edn (British Records Association, 1999), p. 17). Thus a ferling in this context is probably about 7.5 acres. In this manuscript, the surveyor does not provide any clear definition for the term.

[9] Suit of court means he must appear at the manor court of the lady abbess and, if required, serve as a juror.

[10] An amercement is a financial penalty levied by a court (Bailey, *The English Manor*, p. 241).

[11] This may be the Simon Deuenysshe listed in *DLS*, p. 45.

[12] Boon-service or bond-service was compulsory labour provided without payment. It was seasonal in nature (Bailey, *The English Manor*, pp. 30, 241).

.Extent.   .Nytherton.

Et dat de auxilio .ij.*s*. .j.*d*.

And she hands over as tallage 2*s* 1*d*.

* Johannes Pouke Natiuus Domine tenet .j. ferlingum terre apud Poukehegh'
reddendo per annum ad terminos
predictos .iij.*s*. Et arabit dimidiam
acram ad yuernagium et dimidiam
acram ad tremesium et herciabit sine
cibo. Et valet opus Domine .vj.*d*. ob.
cum herciatura. Et arabit de prece per
.j. diem in hyeme et per alium diem
in quadragesima. Et habebit prandium
semel in die si boues habeat. Et valet
opus .vj.*d*. Et herciabit semel de prece
ad yuernagium et habebit prandium, et
semel de prece ad tremesium et habebit
prandium si affros habeat. Et valet opus
Domine .j.*d*. Et herciabit dimidiam acram de consuetudine sine cibo et valet
opus Domine ob. Item debet falcare
.j. acram prati sine cibo et valet opus
Domine .iij.*d*. Et leuabit pratum per .ij.
dimidias dies cum .j. homine et valet
opus Domine *ob. q*. Et tractabit fenum
seu iuuabit ad mullonem feni sine cibo
per dimidiam diem et valet opus ob. Et
metet .xij. acras sine cibo et valet opus
Domine .iij.*s*. Et metet .iiij. bedrypes
cum .j. homine cum cibo bis in die.
Et valet opus Domine .v.*d*. Et faciet
.iiij. averagia cum .j. homine et affro
suo per annum. Et in tanta distancia
quod posset in crastino redire domi.
Et valet opus domine .vj.*d*. Et cum
uenerit apud Legh' habebit cibum. Et
operabit qualibet septimana .j. opus per
.xl. septimanas per dimidiam diem sine
cibo et valet opus domine in toto .xx.*d*.
videlicet quodlibet opus cuiuslibet diei
ob. Et cariabit petram molarem tertio
emptori cum ceteris vicinis suis.

* John Pouke, a villein of the Lady,
holds one ferling of land at Poukehegh'
paying 3*s* per year at the aforementioned terms. And he will plough half
an acre of the winter crop and half an
acre of the spring-sown crop and he
will harrow without food.[13] And the
work with the harrowing is worth 6½*d*
to the Lady. And he will plough for one
day in winter and for one other day in
Lent as boon work. And he will have
dinner once per day if he has the oxen.
And the work is worth 6*d*. And he will
harrow once for the winter crop as
boon work and he will have dinner, and
once as boon work for the spring-sown
crop and he will have dinner if he has
draught animals. And the work is worth
1*d* to the Lady. And he will harrow
half an acre as is the custom and the
work is worth ½*d* to the Lady. Also he
must mow one acre of meadow without
food and the work is worth 3*d* to the
Lady. And he will do hay-making for 2
half-days with one man and the work is
worth ¾*d* to the Lady. And he will turn
the hay or he will help with the stacking of the hay without food for half a
day and the work is worth ½*d*. And he
will reap 12 acres without food and the
work is worth 3*s* to the Lady. And he
will reap for 4 harvest services with one
man, with food twice in the day. And
the work is worth 5*d* to the Lady. And
he will provide 4 carrying services with
one man and with his draught animal
per year, and at such a distance that he
would be able on the next day to return
home. And the work is worth 6*d*.

---

[13] The intention here is that he will not be provided with food, not that he is forbidden to stop
and eat.

Et domina inueniet plaustrum et .ij. boues cum .j. seruiente. Et valent predicta opera in toto .vij.*s.* .j.*d. q.* Et dabit de auxilio post festum sancti Michaelis .ij.*s.* .j.*d.* Et purgabit bedum molendini si Domina voluerit cum ceteris vicinis suis. Et habebit *ob. q.* Et sic nichil valet Domine. Et erit prepositus.

And when he will come to Legh' he will have food. Every week for 40 weeks he will labour at one item of work for half a day without food, and the work is worth 20*d* in total to the Lady, namely whatever task on whatever day ½*d.* And with others of his neighbours he will carry a millstone to the third purchaser.[14] And the Lady will provide the wagon and 2 oxen with one servant. And the aforementioned works are worth in total 7*s* 1¼*d.* And he will give 2*s* 1*d* as tallage after the feast of St Michael. And, if the Lady so wishes, he will clean out the mill-leat with others of his neighbours.[15] And he will have ¾*d.* And thus it is worth nothing to the Lady. And he will be the reeve.[16]

* Henricus Pouke liber corpore tenet .j. ferlingum terre ibidem reddendo ad terminos predictos .iij.*s.*[17] Et faciet omnia seruicia predicta que dictus Johannes facit. Et percipiet eodem modo. Et dat de auxilio .ij.*s.* .j.*d.*

* Henry Pouke, free in body,[18] holds one ferling of land there paying 3*s* at the aforementioned terms. And he will perform all the aforementioned services that the said John does. And he will benefit in the same way. And he hands over 2*s* 1*d* for tallage.

* Johannes atte Hurne liber corpore tenet dimidium ferlingum terre et botlonde reddendo ad terminos predictos .ij.*s.* .j.*d.* ob. Et facit omnia servici sicut dictus Johannes Pouke excepto quod non facit nisi duo averagia. Et dat de auxilio .xij.*d.* ob.

* John atte Hurne, free in body, holds half a ferling of land and botlonde paying 2*s* 1½*d* at the aforementioned terms.[19] And he performs all services as the said John Pouke except that he only performs 2 carrying services. And he hands over 12½*d* for tallage.

* Johannes Matheu liber corpore tenet dimidium ferlingum terre reddendo ad

* John Matheu, free in body, holds half a ferling of land paying at

---

[14] This curious term is discussed in the Introduction.

[15] *Bedum* is normally translated as the mill-dam or mill-pond, but in this circumstance it surely refers more specifically to the mill leat.

[16] The office of reeve was an important one within the medieval manor. Elected annually and by compulsion from within the unfree tenantry, the reeve was usually quit of some or all his rents and services by way of compensation. For a fuller discussion, see Bailey, *The English Manor*, pp. 98–100.

[17] This could be the same person as Henry Pouke in *DLS*, p. 44 (in Colyton Hundred).

[18] The term *liber corpore* (free in body) is discussed in the Introduction. It means that Henry Pouke was not born in serfdom, but he nevertheless has to undertake the obligations that accompany the holding of a bonded tenement. That includes the payment of aid or tallage (*auxilium*).

[19] The term *botlonde* here may be a variation on bond-land (land held by bondage tenure).

.Nytherton.

terminos predictos .xviij.*d.* Et facit omnia seruicia sicut dictus Johannes atte
Hurne. Et dat de auxilio .xij.*d.* ob.

* Radulphus Dauy liber corpore tenet
.j. ferlingum terre reddendo ad terminos
predictos .v.*s.* Et arabit dimidiam acram
ad yuernagium et dimidiam acram ad
tremesium et herciabit sine cibo. Et
valet opus Domine .vj.*d.* ob. Et arabit
per .ij. dies de prece cum cibo si boues
habeat. Et valet opus Domine .vj.*d.* Et
herciabit per .ij. dies de prece si affros
habeat et habebit prandium. Et valet
opus .j.*d.* et herciabit dimidiam acram
de consuetudine sine cibo et valet
opus ob. Et metet per .iiij. dies cum .j.
homine et habebit prandium bis in die.
Et valet opus Domine .v.*d.* Et iuuabit
ad mullonem feni et valet opus ob. Et
mundabit bedum molendini cum ceteris
vicinis sicut prius dictum est. Et cariabit petram molarem cum ceteris vicinis
suis ut supra. Et dat de auxilio .ij.*s.* .j.*d.*

the aforementioned terms 18*d.* And he
performs all the services as the said
John atte Hurne. And he hands over
12½*d* as tallage.

* Ralph Davy, free in body, holds one
ferling of land paying 5*s* at the aforementioned terms. And he will plough
half an acre for the winter crop and half
an acre for the spring-sown crop and he
will harrow without food. And the work
is worth 6½*d* to the Lady. And he will
plough for 2 days as boon-service with
food if he has the oxen. And the work is
worth 6*d* to the Lady. And he will harrow for 2 days as boon-service if he has
the draught animals and he will have
dinner. And the work is worth 1*d*, and
he will harrow as is customary without
food and the work is worth ½*d*. And
he will reap for 4 days with one man
and he will have dinner twice in the
day. And the work is worth 5*d* to the
Lady. And he will help with stacking
the hay and the work is worth ½*d*. And
he will clean the mill-leat with other
neighbours as said previously. And he
will carry the millstone with others of
his neighbours as above. And he hands
over 2*s* 1*d* as tallage.

* Nicholaus Matheu tenet .j. tenementum et .vj. acras terre reddendo ad
terminos predictos .xviij.*d.* Et arabit
per .ij. dies de prece si boues habeat. Et
habebit prandium et valet opus .vj.*d.* Et
metet per .iiij. dies cum .j. homine et
habebit prandium. Et valet opus domine
.v.*d.* Et herciabit per .ij. dies de prece
si affros habeat et habebit prandium
et valet opus Domine .j.*d.* Et herciabit
dimidiam acram de iure et valet opus
ob. Et iuuabit ad mullonem feni et valet
opus ob. Et iuuabit ad bedum molendini et cariagium petram molarem ut
supra. Et dat de auxilio .vj.*d. q.*

* Nicholas Matheu holds one tenement
and 6 acres of land paying 18*d* at the
aforementioned terms. And he will
plough for 2 days as boon-service if he
has the oxen. And he will have dinner
and the work is worth 6*d*. And he will
reap for 4 days with one man and he
will have dinner. And the work is worth
6*d* to the Lady. And he will harrow
for 2 days as boon-service if he has
the draught animals and he will have
dinner and the work is worth 1*d* to the
Lady. And he will harrow half an acre
by right and the work is worth ½*d*. And
he will help with the stacking of the
hay and the work is worth ½*d*. And he
will help with the mill-leat and carrying
the mill stone as above. And he hands
over 6¼*d* as tallage.

¶ Et sciendum est quod quilibet predic-
torum in Bondagio erit prepositus si sit
electus. Et tunc erit quietus de omnibus
redditibus et seruiciis suis. Non potest
filium suum ponere ad literaturam nec
filiam suam maritare nec pullanum
masculum sibi pullonatum vel bouem
sibi vitulatum sine licencia Dominarum
vendere.

¶ And it is understood that any of the
aforementioned in bondage will be the
reeve if he be elected. And then he will
be quit of all his rents and services. He
may not educate his son nor give his
daughter in marriage nor sell a young
male horse that has been foaled to him
or an ox that has been calved to him
without licence of the Ladies.[20]

* Item Thomas Clanefelde tenet .j.co-
tagium et .j. acram terre et dimidiam
acram prati reddendo per annum .ij.*s*
.iij.*d.* Et metet .j. acram. Et valet opus
.iij.*d.* Et iuuabit ad mullonem feni et
valet

Also Thomas Clanefelde holds one
cottage and one acre of land and half an
acre of meadow paying 2*s* 3*d* per year.
And he will reap one acre. And the
work is worth 3*d*. And he will help with
the stacking of the hay and

[20] For a very similar passage, see *Custumals of the Manors of Laughton, Willingdon, and Goring*, ed. by A. E. Wilson, Sussex Record Society Publications, 60 (Sussex Record Society, 1961), p. 71.

.Extent.

opus obolus. Et dat de auxilio .j.*d. ob. q.*

* Galfridus Rinel tenet .j. cotagium et .j. acram terre reddendo per annum .xij.*d.*[21] Et metet .j. acram terre et valet opus .iij.*d.* Et iuuabit ad mullonem feni et valet opus ob. Et dat de auxilio .ij.*d. q.*

* Philippus Kymer tenet .j. cotagium cum curtilagio reddendo per annum .xvj.*d.* Et metet .j. acram et valet opus .iij.*d.* Et iuuabit ad mullonem feni faciendum et valet opus ob. Et dabit de auxilio .j.*d.*

* Matilda Turnour tenet .j. cotagium cum curtilagio reddendo per annum .xv.*d.* pro omnibus seruiciis.

* Agnes relicta fabri tenet .j. cotagium et .j. acram terre reddendo per annum .ij.*s.* .iiij.*d.* Et metet .j. acram. Et valet opus .iij.*d.* Et dat de auxilio .j.*d.* ob.

* Robertus Turnour tenet .j. cotagium cum curtilagio reddendo per annum .xviij.*d.* Et metet .j. acram. Et valet opus .iij.*d.*

* Ricardus Spynke tenet .j. cotagium reddendo per annum .xij.*d.* Et metet .j. acram et valet opus .iij.*d.*

* Johannes Faber tenet .j. tenementum cum dimidiam acram prati reddendo per annum .iij.*s.* pro omnibus seruiciis.

* Alicia Couple tenet .j. cotagium reddendo per annum .xij.*d.* Et metet .j. acram. Et valet opus .iij.*d.*

the work is worth ½*d*. And he hands over 1¾*d* as tallage.

* Geoffrey Rinel holds one cottage and one acre of land paying 12*d* per year. And he will reap one acre of land and the work is worth 3*d*. And he will help with the stacking of the hay and the work is worth ½*d*. And he hands over 2¼*d* as tallage.

* Philip Kymer holds one cottage with a curtilage paying 15*d* per year. And he will reap one acre and the work is worth 3*d*. And he will help with the stacking of the hay and the work is worth ½*d*. And he will give 1*d* as tallage.

* Matilda Turnour holds one cottage with a curtilage paying 15*d* per year for all services.

* Agnes the widow of the smith holds one cottage and one acre of land paying 2*s* 3*d* per year. And she will reap one acre. And the work is worth 3*d*. And she hands over a 1½*d* as tallage.

* Robert Turnour holds one cottage with a curtilage paying 18*d* per year. And he will reap one acre. And the work is worth 3*d*.

* Richard Spynke holds one cottage paying 12*d* per year. And he will reap one acre and the work is worth 3*d*.

* John Smith [*Faber*] holds one tenement with half an acre of meadow paying 3*s* per year for all services.

* Alice Couple holds one cottage paying 12*d* per year. And she will reap one acre. And the work is worth 3*d*.

---

[21] This tenant's surname appears to be spelled as 'Rinel', but it is possible that the scribe's 'n' is an oddly formed 'u'. Thus the surname may be Riuel ('Rivel' in modern terms).

* Willelmus atte Hurne tenet .j. cotagium cum curtilagio reddendo per annum .xv.*d.* pro omnibus seruiciis.

* Walterus Batyn tenet .j. cotagium et .ij. acras terre reddendo per annum .iij. .*s.* .vj.*d.* Et metet .j. acram. Et valet opus .iij.*d.*

* Tenementum Pypere est in manu Domine quod consueuit reddere .xv.*d.* pro omnibus seruiciis.

* Curtilagium fabrice est in manu domine quod consueuit reddere .ix.*d.* pro omnibus seruiciis quod quidem curtilagium Rogerus Faber aliquando tenuit.

¶ Summa totius redditus tam liberorum quam villanorum .Lxj.*s.* ob.

* William atte Hurne holds one cottage with a curtilage paying 15*d* per year for all services.

* Walter Batyn holds one cottage and 2 acres paying 3*s* 6*d* per year. And he will reap one acre. And the work is worth 3*d*.

* The Pypere tenement that used to yield 15*d* for all services is in the hand of the Lady.

* The curtilage of the smith that Roger Smith [*Faber*] used to hold and which used to yield 9*d* for all services, is in the hand of the Lady.

¶ The sum of all the rent whether of freemen or of villeins [is] 61*s* ½*d*.

.Netherton.

[fol. 142v]

¶ Summa auxilii villanorum ibidem .xij.*s.*

¶ Summa valoris seruiciorum et operum dicti homagii si boues habeant .xxxiiij*s.* .viij.*d.*

¶ Summa valoris totius dominici per extentam predictam .ix.*li.* .vij.*s.* .ij.*d.* ob.

¶ Memorandum quod in hoc manerio sunt in decasu .ij.*d.* ob. quos heredes Thome de Bromleghe et heredes Iordani de Wyteleghe reddere deberent, sicut apparet per cartas in Nythertone super numeros .x. et .xj.

¶ The sum of the tallage of the villeins there [is] 12*s*.

¶ The sum of the value of the services and works of the said tenantry if they have oxen is 34*s* 8*d*.

¶ The sum of the total value of the demesne in the aforementioned extent £9 7*s* 2½*d*.

¶ Note that in this manor there are in decay[22] the 2½*d* that the heirs of Thomas de Bromleghe and the heirs of Jordan de Wyteleghe ought to pay, as is certainly evident through the charters for Netherton at numbers X and XI.[23]

---

[22] 'In decay' meaning income that is lost or has to be written off.
[23] *Cartulary*, items 164 and 165 on pp. 60–1.

* Item memorandum quod hoc manerium oneratur de communi secta ad
hundredum de Colytone que communit-
er redimitur pro .iij.*s.* .iiij.*d* annuatim.

* Also note that this manor is burdened
with suit of court at the hundred of
Colyton which is normally bought off
for 3*s* 4*d* annually.

* Item oneratur predictum manerium
de .j.*li.* cere prece communiter .vij.*d.*
Et de .iiij.*d.* annuis solvendis Abbati de
Quarreria et Johanni de Pultymor pro
terra de Swetrygge et communia super
terram de Wyteleghe sicut apparet
per cartam Rogeri de Pultimor super
numerum .v.

* Also the aforementioned manor
is burdened with one pound of wax
usually priced at 7*d*, and of 4*d*, owing annually to the Abbot of Quarr[24]
and to John of Pultymor for the land
of Swetrygge and the common on
the land of Wyteleghe as is certainly
evident through the charter of Roger of
Pultimor at number V.[25]

* Item oneratur de .j.*d.* annui redditus
solvendo in festo sancti Michaelis
Dominis de Colewylle, sicut apparet
per cartam Willelmi de Colewille super
numerum .iij.

* Also [the abbey] is burdened with
1*d* of annual rent owing on the feast of
Saint Michael to the lords of Colewylle,
as is certainly evident through the charter of William de Colewille at number
III.[26]

* Item oneratur de Regali seruicio quod
appelatur Horderisyne annuatim de .j.
ob.

* Also it is burdened with the royal
service named Horderisyne annually
for 1½*d*.[27]

¶ Et sic valet manerium de Claro per
extentam predictam deductur oneribus
supradictis .ix.*li* .ij.*s* .vij.*d* ob.

* And thus the manor, with all the
aforementioned burdens deducted, is
worth, net, £9 2*s* 7½*d* in the aforementioned extent

[Now follows a much later note in a
cursive hand. At least part of it was
added no earlier than November 1503]

---

[24] The Cistercian Abbey of Quarr was founded in the first half of the twelfth century on the Isle of Wight (Knowles, *Medieval Religious Houses*, p. 113). Some lands held of Quarr had been granted to the canons when they were resident at Canonsleigh (*Cartulary*, items 159 and 182).

[25] *Cartulary*, item 159, pp. 58–9. Polimore lay in the parish of Farway (*Cartulary*, p. xxvii).

[26] *Cartulary*, item 157, p. 58. The lands of Colwell lay in the parish of Farway (ibid., p. xxvii).

[27] For discussion of a similar term once used in Devon (horderesgeve), see R. E. Latham, 'Curia Tremure', *The English Historical Review* 71 (1956), pp. 428–33 (p. 431).

Homages

Memorandum quod die Luna proxima ante festum sancti Martini anno regni regis henrici quarti undecimo Johannes filius et heres Agnetis Hurne fecit homagium suum Lucie Abbatisse de Canonleghe apud Canonleghe pro tenementis que de domina tenet in Stowey ut de Manerio suo de Nytherton'.

* Item Ricardus Hurne fecit domine Johanne Arundelle Abbatisse de Canonleghe homagium ibidem pro terris et tenementis predictis decimo die Nouembris anno regni regis Edwardi quarti sexto.

* Item Willelmus Russelle fecit Domine Elisabethe Fouhelle abbatisse de Canonleghe homagium suum ibidem pro terris et tenementis vocatis Stowey quod de domina tenet de predicto manerio xij die Nouembris anno regni regis henrici septimo undevicesimo.

Note that on the Monday next before the feast of St Martin in the eleventh year of the reign of King Henry IV,[28] John the son and heir of Agnes Hurne made his homage to Lucy the abbess of Canonleghe at Canonleghe for the tenements that he holds from the Lady in Stowey as from her manor of Netherton.

* Also Richard Hurne made homage there to the Lady Joan Arundelle Abbess of Canonleghe for the lands and tenements aforementioned, on the tenth day of November in the sixth year of the reign of King Edward IV.[29]

* Also William Russelle made his homage there to the Lady Elizabeth Fouhelle Abbess of Canonsleigh for the lands and tenements called Stowey that he holds from the Lady from the aforementioned manor, on the twelfth day of November in the nineteenth year of the reign of King Henry VII.[30]

---

[28] This would equate to Monday, 4 November 1409. The lengthy abbacy of Lucy Warr ended with her death on 11 October 1410 (see *Cartulary,* p. 117 for the list of abbesses; also Smith and London, pp. 549–50; David M. Smith, *The Heads of Religious Houses England and Wales. 3, 1377–1540* (Cambridge University Press, 2008), pp. 634–5).

[29] Monday, 10 November 1466.

[30] Sunday, 12 November 1503.

Glossary[1]

Advowson: See **patron**

Amercement: A financial penalty levied by a court

Appropriation: To transfer the endowment, or part of the endowment, of a parish church to a religious institution

Assart: Land recently cleared for cultivation

At will or **tenant-at-will:** An insecure tenure where the tenant paid a cash rent but had no right to pass on the holding to their heirs. The tenancy might be terminated by the lord or lady 'at will'

Auxilium: See **tallage**

Bailiff: The local official responsible for the day-to-day management of the manor. The bailiff performed a similar job to the **reeve**, but the bailiff was salaried

Bondage: The position or condition of a **serf**; servitude, serfdom

Boonwork: A seasonal labour service owed on the **demesne** of the lord or lady, often attracting the provision of food and ale by them. It originated as a free will service, or 'boon', to the lord or lady

Bushel: A dry measure of 8 gallons for grain and fruit especially

Cartulary: A book containing copies of deeds, charters and other legal records

Charter: A legal document recording the grant of land or privileges

Close: A small plot of land (from the Latin *clauwa*)

Cottager or cottar: An unfree smallholder

Croft: An enclosed plot of land often adjacent to a dwelling house

Curtilage: See **messuage**

Custumal: A medieval document listing the tenants of a particular manor and the conditions of their tenure, esp. the services owed to their lord

Customary tenant: An unfree tenant whose obligations and terms of tenure are determined and enforced in the manor court; also known as **villein** tenure

Customary tenure: Defined in the courts of the common law as unfree tenure whose obligations and terms were determined and enforced in the manor court; also known as **villein** tenure

---

[1] Many of the entries in this glossary are taken from Mark Bailey, *The English Manor, c. 1200–1500*, Manchester Medieval Sources Series (Manchester University Press, 2002), pp. 241–47. See also p. 3 where Bailey provides his definition of what constituted a manor in the later medieval period.

Demesne: The land within a manor allocated to the lord or lady for their own use

Dower: The widow's right to hold a proportion (normally one-third) of her deceased husband's land for the rest of her life

Endowment: The properties that a religious house was granted to provide its income. These could be manors or churches as well as mills, the right to hold markets or fairs, and sundry other items

Enfeoff: To grant land as a **fief**

Extent: A survey of a manor, its **demesne** and tenantry, providing a valuation of its lands and services. The valuation was the annual amount that could be obtained for those resources if they were leased out

Farm or **At farm:** A fixed sum paid for leasing a resource such as land or a mill

Farmer: A lessee who holds some property at **farm**

Fealty: An oath of fidelity sworn by a new tenant to the lord in recognition of his obligations

Ferling: A measurement of land area, a quarter-**virgate** (nominally 7.5 acres)

Fief, fee: Hereditary land held from a superior lord in return for **homage** and (often military) service

Fine: A money payment to the lord or lady to obtain a specific concession

Frankpledge: A group of men (often a set of twelve) bound together by mutual surety to bring criminals and malefactors to justice and report on criminal and civil issues. See also the **leet court**

Glebe: The landed endowment of a parish church

Hearth-penny or **Hearth-silver:** An annual tax levied on householders; also known as Peter's Penny

Heriot: A death duty, normally the best beast, levied by the manorial lord or lady on the estate of a deceased tenant

Hide: An Anglo-Saxon land measurement, notionally 120 acres

Homage: The act by which a vassal acknowledges a superior lord or lady

Hundred: The unit of local government between the county and the vill

Leet court or court leet: The court of a vill whose **view of frankpledge** had been franchised to a local lord or lady by the Crown

Letters patent: An open letter or document issued by a monarch or government to record a contract, authorise or command an action, or confer a privilege, right, office, title, or property

Malt silver or **malt money:** Money paid as a tax on the making of malt

Manor: A territorial unit of lordship and the basic unit for the lord's estate administration. As well as the land and its tenants, other economic resources might include mills, fisheries, mineral rights etc.

Merchet: A fine paid by **villein** tenants to their manorial lord for permission for one of their children to marry (normally a daughter)

Messuage: A plot of land containing a dwelling house and outbuildings

Moiety: Usually a half, one of two equal parts

Patron: The person or organisation (e.g. the abbey) holding the right to appoint a clerk as rector or vicar of a parish church. The right is called the **advowson**. This right could be loaned out or might be divided among several patrons

Perquisites: Income coming to the lord or lady from rights, **fines** and **amercements**

Reeve: The local official responsible for the day-to-day management of the **manor**. The reeve performed a similar job to the **bailiff**, but the reeve was elected from the manorial tenantry

Relief: The payment made by a free tenant on entering a holding

Seisin: Possession (of land)

Serf: An unfree peasant characterised by onerous personal servility

Sheriff: An official responsible for the administration of a county by the Crown (i.e. the shire **reeve**)

Socage: A form of tenure of peasant land, normally free, including **suit of court**

Suit of court: The right and obligation to attend a court; the individual so attending is a suitor

Tallage: The right of the lord or lady of the manor to tax unfree peasants at will

Tenement: A landholding

Tithe: A tenth of annual produce or earnings, taken as a tax (originally in kind) for the support of the church and clergy

Tithing-man: The chief member of a tithing (i.e. group of men) in the system of **frankpledge**

View of frankpledge: See **frankpledge**

Villein: A peasant whose freedom of time and action is constrained by his or her lord or lady; a villein was not able to use the royal courts

Virgate: A quarter of a **hide**; a standardised **villein** holding of around 30 acres. Also known as a yardland. Sometimes it is used to mean a yard measure.

Vill: The local unit of civil administration

BIBLIOGRAPHY

1. UNPUBLISHED PRIMARY SOURCES

Chelmsford, Essex Record Office

'Extracts from Records Relating to Mistley and Manningtree, 1085–1693'. n.d., T/P 51/1.

'Miscellaneous Papers Relating to the County of Essex'. n.d., D/Dcm Z19

'Transcript and Translation of Survey of Manor of Schydyngho, 1323', T/P 64/11.

Exeter, Devon Heritage Centre

'Dunsford Court Rolls'. 1552, 6327M/M/1.

'Farway Court Roll'. May 1534, CR/532.

2. PUBLISHED PRIMARY SOURCES

Calendar of Entries in the Papal Registers Relating to Great Britain and Ireland: Papal Letters. Vol. 1. London: HMSO, 1893.

Calendar of the Patent Rolls, Edward VI, Vol. 3, 1549–1551. London: HMSO, 1925.

Calendar of Inquisitions Post Mortem and Other Analogous Documents Preserved in the Public Record Office. Vol. 25, 16–20, Henry VI (1437–1442). Calendar of Inquisitions Post Mortem and Other Analogous Documents Preserved in the Public Record Office. New Series; v. 25. Woodbridge: Boydell Press, 2009.

Erskine, Audrey M. *The Devonshire Lay Subsidy of 1332*. Devon and Cornwall Record Society Publications. New Series 14. Torquay: Devon and Cornwall Record Society, 1969.

Ewen, C. L'Estrange, ed. *Devon Taxation Returns in 1334*. Paignton: Printed for the Author, 1939.

Farr, M. W. *Accounts and Surveys of the Wiltshire Lands of Adam de Stratton*. Vol. 14. Devizes: Wiltshire Archaeological and Natural History Society Records Branch, 1959.

Fox, Harold S. A., and Oliver James Padel, eds. *The Cornish Lands of the Arundells of Lanherne, Fourteenth to Sixteenth Centuries*. Devon and Cornwall Record Society Publications 41. Exeter: Devon and Cornwall Record Society, 2000.

Green, Emanuel. *Pedes Finum, Commonly Called Feet of Fines, for the County of Somerset*. Vol. 6. Somerset Record Society. Somerset: Somerset Record Society, 1892.

Hart, William Henry, and Ponsonby A. Lyons, eds. *Cartularium Monasterii de*

Rameseia. Vol. 1. 3 vols. Cambridge Library Collection. Rolls. London: Longman, 1884.

Harvey, P. D. A. *Manorial Records of Cuxham, Oxfordshire, c.1200–1359*. Oxfordshire Record Series 50. Oxfordshire Record Society, 1976.

Hingeston-Randolph, F. C., ed. *The Register of Edmund Stafford (A.D. 1395–1419): An Index and Abstract of Its Contents*. Exeter: Eland, 1886.

———, ed. *The Register of John de Grandisson, Bishop of Exeter, (A.D. 1327–1369)*. 3 vols. London: George Bell & Sons, 1894.

———, ed. *The Register of Walter de Stapeldon, Bishop of Exeter (A.D. 1307–1326)*. London: G. Bell, 1892.

———, ed. *The Registers of Walter Bronescombe (A.D. 1257–1280), and Peter Quivil (A.D. 1280–1291), Bishops of Exeter, with Some Records of the Episcopate of Bishop Thomas de Bytton (A.D. 1291–1307); Also the Taxation of Pope Nicholas IV. A.D. 1291 – (Diocese of Exeter)*. Episcopal Registers of the Diocese of Exeter. London: George Bell & Sons, York Street, Covent Garden, 1889.

'Inquisitions Post Mortem, Edward II, File 64 | British History Online'. Accessed 19 February 2025. https://www.british-history.ac.uk/inquis-post-mortem/vol6/pp129-139.

'Inquisitions Post Mortem, Edward III, File 130 | British History Online'. Accessed 19 February 2025. https://www.british-history.ac.uk/inquis-post-mortem/vol10/pp194-209.

'Inquisitions Post Mortem, Richard II, File 67 | British History Online'. Accessed 19 February 2025. https://www.british-history.ac.uk/inquis-post-mortem/vol16/pp407-425.

London, Vera C. M., ed. *The Cartulary of Canonsleigh Abbey: Harleian MS.No.3660. A Calendar*. Devon and Cornwall Record Society Publications 8. Torquay: Devon and Cornwall Record Society, 1965.

Maxwell-Lyte, H. C., ed. *Two Registers Formerly Belonging to the Family of Beauchamp of Hatch*. Somerset Record Society 35. Frome: Somerset Record Society, 1920.

Stacy, Neil E., and British Academy, eds. *Surveys of the Estates of Glastonbury Abbey c.1135–1201*. Records of Social and Economic History 33. Oxford: Oxford University Press, 2001.

Taxatio Ecclesiastica Angliae et Walliae Auctoritate P. Nicholai IV. circa A.D. 1291. London: George Eyre and Andrew Strahan, 1802.

Valor Ecclesiasticus, Temp. Henr. VIII. Auctoritate Regia Institutus. 6 vols. Record Commissioners Publications. London: George Eyre and Andrew Strahan, 1810.

Ward, Jennifer C. and Essex Record Office. *The Medieval Essex Community: The Lay Subsidy of 1327*. Essex Historical Documents 1. Essex: Essex Record Office, 1983.

Wells-Furby, Bridget. *The Berkeley Estate 1281–1417: Its Economy and Development*. Bristol and Gloucestershire Monographs; No. 1. Bristol: Gloucestershire Archaeological Society, 2012.

Wilson, A. E., ed. *Custumals of the Manors of Laughton, Willingdon, and Goring*. Sussex Record Society Publications 60. Lewes: Sussex Record Society, 1961.

Youings, Joyce. *Devon Monastic Lands: Calendar of Particulars for Grants 1536–1558*. NED-New edition. Vol. 1. Devon & Cornwall Record Society. [Publications] New Ser. United Kingdom: Boydell & Brewer, 1955.

3. SECONDARY SOURCES

Alcock, N. W. 'An East Devon Manor in the Later Middle Ages: Part 1'. *Transactions of the Devonshire Association* 102 (1950): 141–88.

Ashdowne, Richard. *Dictionary of Medieval Latin from British Sources*. Oxford: Published for the British Academy by Oxford University Press, 2018.

Atkinson, Desmond Paul. 'Canonsleigh Abbey: A Thriving Devon Nunnery?' *Ex Historia* 7 (2015): 1–36.

Bailey, Mark. *The English Manor, c.1200–1500*. Manchester Medieval Sources Series. Manchester: Manchester University Press, 2002.

———. *Medieval Suffolk: An Economic and Social History, 1200–1500*. Woodbridge: Boydell & Brewer, 2007.

———. 'The Transformation of Customary Tenures in Southern England, *c*. 1350 to *c*. 1500'. *Agricultural History Review* 62, no. 2 (2014): 210–30.

Beresford, Maurice. *English Medieval Boroughs: A Hand-List*. Newton Abbot: David and Charles, 1973.

Britnell, R. H. 'Essex Markets before 1350'. *Essex Archaeology and History* 13 (1981): 15–21.

Butlin, R. A. 'Some Terms Used in Agrarian History: A Glossary'. *The Agricultural History Review* 9, no. 2 (1961): 98–104.

Campbell, B. M. S. *The Great Transition: Climate, Disease and Society in the Late Medieval World*. Cambridge: Cambridge University Press, 2016.

Campbell, Bruce M. S. *English Seigniorial Agriculture, 1250–1450*. Cambridge Studies in Historical Geography 31. Cambridge: Cambridge University Press, 2000.

Campbell, Bruce M. S., James A. Galloway and Margaret Murphy. 'Rural Land-Use in the Metropolitan Hinterland, 1270–1339: The Evidence of "Inquisitiones Post Mortem"'. *The Agricultural History Review* 40, no. 1 (1992): 1–22.

Cheney, C. R., and Michael Jones. *A Handbook of Dates for Students of British History*. New edn. Royal Historical Society Guides and Handbooks; No. 4. Cambridge: Cambridge University Press, 2000.

Cherry, Bridget. *The Buildings of England. Devon / by Bridget Cherry and Nikolaus Pevsner*. New Haven: Yale University Press, 2004.

Dockray-Miller, Mary. *Saints Edith and Æthelthryth: Princesses, Miracle Workers, and Their Late Medieval Audience: The Wilton Chronicle and The Wilton Life of St Æthelthryth*. Medieval Women: Texts and Contexts; vol. 25. Turnhout: Brepols, 2009.

Dugdale, William. *Monasticon Anglicanum: A History of the Abbies and Other Monasteries ... and Cathedral and Collegiate Churches ... in England and Wales.* New edn by John Caley, Henry Ellis and Bulkeley Bandinel. 8 vols. London: Longman, Hurst, 1817.

Ellis, Mary. *Using Manorial Records.* Rev. edn. Readers' Guides/Great Britain. Public Record Office, no. 6. London: PRO Publications in association with the Royal Commission on Historical Manuscripts, 1997.

Elworthy, F. T. 'Canonsleigh'. *Reports and Transactions of the Devonshire Association* 24 (1892): 359–76.

Emden, A. B. *A Biographical Register of the University of Cambridge to 1500.* Cambridge: Cambridge University Press, 1963.

———. *A Biographical Register of the University of Oxford to A.D. 1500.* 3 vols. Oxford: Clarendon Press, 1957–9.

Farmer, David. 'Millstones for Medieval Manors'. *Agricultural History Review* 40 (1992): 97–111.

Feiling, K. G. 'An Essex Manor in the Fourteenth Century'. *The English Historical Review* 26 (1911): 333–8.

Finberg, H. P. R. *Tavistock Abbey: A Study in the Social and Economic History of Devon.* New York: Kelley, 1969.

Fisher, J. L. *A Medieval Farming Glossary of Latin and English Words Taken Mainly from Essex Records.* London: National Council of Social Service for the Standing Conference for Local History, 1968.

Fowler, R. C. 'Religious Gilds of Essex'. *Transactions of the Essex Archaeological Society*, New Series, 16 (1923): 59–60.

Hall, David. *The Open Fields of England.* 1st edn. Medieval History and Archaeology. Oxford: Oxford University Press, 2014. https://doi.org/10.1093/acprof:oso/9780198702955.001.0001.

Harvey, P. D. A. *Manorial Records.* Rev. edn. Archives and the User 5. London: British Records Association, 1999.

Heale, Martin. *The Dependent Priories of Medieval English Monasteries.* 1st edn. Vol. 22. Studies in the History of Medieval Religion. Woodbridge: Boydell & Brewer, 2004.

Holt, Richard. *The Mills of Medieval England.* Oxford: Basil Blackwell, 1988.

Hoskins, W. G. *Devon.* Chichester: Phillimore, 2003.

Hoskins, W. G., and H. P. R. Finberg. *Devonshire Studies.* London: Cape, 1952.

Ison, J. R. 'Canonsleigh: I–VI'. *Tiverton Civic Society Newsletter*, April 1984–November 1985.

Jenkins, John Christopher. 'Torre Abbey: Locality, Community and Society in Medieval Devon'. Doctoral thesis, University of Oxford, 2010.

Jones, Sarah Ruth Rees. 'Property, Tenure and Rents: Some Aspects of the Topography and Economy of Medieval York'. Doctoral thesis, University of York, 1987.

Jurkowski, M., Nigel Ramsay, Simon Renton and List and Index Society. *English Monastic Estates, 1066–1540: A List of Manors, Churches and Chapels*. 3 vols. Special Series; vols 40–2. Kew: List and Index Society, 2007.

Kaye, J. M. *Medieval English Conveyances*. 1st edn. Cambridge Studies in English Legal History. Cambridge: Cambridge University Press, 2009. https://doi.org/10.1017/CBO9780511642241.

Kershaw, I. 'The Great Famine and Agrarian Crisis in England 1315–1322'. In *Peasants, Knights and Heretics: Studies in Medieval English Social History*, edited by R. H. Hilton, 85–132. Cambridge: Cambridge University Press, 1976.

Knowles, David, and R. Neville Hadcock. *Medieval Religious Houses, England and Wales*. London: Longmans, Green, 1953.

Kosminsky, E. A. *Studies in the Agrarian History of England in the Thirteenth Century*. Edited by R. H. Hilton. Translated by Ruth Kisch. Studies in Mediaeval History; No. 8. Oxford: Blackwell, 1956.

Langdon, John. *Mills in the Medieval Economy: England, 1300–1540*. 1st edn. Oxford Scholarship Online. Oxford: Oxford University Press, 2004.

Latham, R. E. 'Curia Tremure'. *The English Historical Review* 71 (1956): 428–33.

———. *Revised Medieval Latin Word-List from British and Irish Sources*. London: Oxford University Press, 1965.

Lennard, R. 'What Is a Manorial Extent?' *The English Historical Review* 44, no. 174 (1929): 256–63.

Lomas, T. 'The Manorial Extent'. *Journal of the Society of Archivists* 6, no. 5 (1980): 260–73.

MacCulloch, Diarmaid. *Thomas Cromwell: A Life*. London: Allen Lane, 2018.

Martin, C. T. *The Record Interpreter: A Collection of Abbreviations, Latin Words and Names Used in English Historical Manuscripts and Records*. London: Reeves & Turner, 1892.

Maxwell-Lyte, H. C. *A History of Dunster and of the Families of Mohun and Luttrell*. Vol. 1. 2 vols. London: St Catherine Press, 1909.

Miller, Edward. *Medieval England: Rural Society and Economic Change, 1086–1348*. Repr. edn, with Corrections. Social and Economic History of England. London: Longman, 1980.

Moore, Andrew. 'Manorial Regulation and Negotiation in a Late Medieval Environment: Land and Community at Herstmonceux, 1308–1440'. Doctoral thesis, University of Waterloo, Ontario, 2021.

Mullan, John. *Land and Family: Trends and Local Variations in the Peasant Land Market on the Winchester Bishopric Estates, 1263–1415*. Studies in Regional and Local History (Hertfordshire, England); vol. 8. Hatfield: University of Hertfordshire Press, 2010.

Page, William. *The Victoria History of the County of Dorset: Volume 2*. Victoria History of the Counties of England. London: Constable, 1908.

Park, Peter B. *My Ancestors Were Manorial Tenants*. New edn. London: Society of Genealogists, 2002.

Polwhele, Richard. *The History of Devonshire*. Exeter: Printed by Trewman and Son, for Cadell, Johnson, and Dilly, London, 1793.

Poos, L. R. *A Rural Society after the Black Death: Essex 1350–1525*. Cambridge Studies in Population, Economy, and Society in Past Time 18. Cambridge: Cambridge University Press, 1991.

Power, Eileen. *Medieval English Nunneries: c. 1275 to 1535*. Cambridge: Cambridge University Press, 1922.

Powicke, F. M. Review of *Curia Regis Rolls of the Reigns of Richard I and John, Preserved in the Public Record Office. Vol. i, Richard I–2 John*, by C. T. Flower. *The English Historical Review* 39, no. 154 (1924): 264–72.

Raban, Sandra. *A Second Domesday? The Hundred Rolls of 1279–80*. Oxford: Oxford University Press, 2004.

Razi, Zvi, and Richard Michael Smith, eds. *Medieval Society and the Manor Court*. Oxford: Clarendon Press, 1996.

Rigby, S. H. *English Society in the Later Middle Ages Class, Status and Gender*. London: Macmillan Education UK, 1995.

Roberts, Jane. *Guide to Scripts Used in English Writings up to 1500*. Corrected edn. Exeter Medieval Texts and Studies. Liverpool: Liverpool University Press, 2015.

Schofield, Phillipp R. *Peasant and Community in Medieval England, 1200–1500*. Medieval Culture and Society. Basingstoke: Palgrave Macmillan, 2003.

Smith, David M. *The Heads of Religious Houses: England and Wales III, 1377–1540*. New York: Cambridge University Press, 2008.

Smith, David M., and Vera C. M. London. *The Heads of Religious Houses: England and Wales II, 1216–1377*. 1st edn. The Heads of Religious Houses Series. Cambridge: Cambridge University Press, 2001.

Smith, R. M. 'Women's Property Rights under Customary Law: Some Developments in the Thirteenth and Fourteenth Centuries'. *Transactions of the Royal Historical Society* 36 (1986): 165–94.

Snell, Lawrence S. *The Suppression of the Religious Foundations of Devon and Cornwall*. Marazion: Wordens of Cornwall Limited, 1967.

Stuart, Denis. *Manorial Records: An Introduction to Their Transcription and Translation*. Chichester: Phillimore, 1992.

Torrance, John. 'Branscombe 1280–1340: An East Devon Manor before the Black Death'. *The Devon Historian* 81 (2012): 67–80.

Ugawa, K. 'The Economic Development of Some Devon Manors in the Thirteenth Century'. *Transactions of the Devonshire Association* 94 (1962): 630–83.

Wells-Furby, Bridget. *The Berkeley Estate 1281–1417: Its Economy and Development*. Bristol and Gloucestershire Monographs; No. 1. Bristol: Gloucestershire Archaeological Society, 2012.

Index of Surnames

Modern forms of names have been used where possible, but the original forms are included and cross-referenced where appropriate. Occupations, offices and titles are cross-referenced to the names of individuals holding them. The scribe is not consistent in his spelling of surnames that begin with 'Atte'. Sometimes he writes 'atte Slade' and at other times 'Atteslade'. All instances are treated as two words here: 'Slade, <first name> atte'. No attempt has been made to indicate whether a name occurs more than once on a particular page – something for the reader to consider. Appendix 1 is not captured in this index because the relevant index entries are already provided for the extent of the manor of Netherton.

Abbreviations: archbp–archbishop; b.–brother; bp–bishop; d.–daughter; gd.–granddaughter; gs.–grandson; n.–note; pr.–prior; s.–son; w.–wife; wid.–widow

Adam
  Robert, heirs of   116
  William   101, 102, 110, 116
Agnes, wid. of the smith (w. of Roger?)   89
Aleyn, Robert   80, 82, 83
Alfeld, Thomas   41, 111, 113
Alforde, Richard   79
Allesford, John de, w. of   111
Aluard, William   51, 66
Anneys, Peter, heirs of   124
Arunde, Andrew   45, 120
Arundel (Arundelle)
  Arundela, d. of John   32
  Joan, abbess of Canonsleigh   91
  Joan, d. of John   32
  John de, heirs of   56
  John   57
  John, s. of Nicholas   32
  Martin   56
  Nicholas   32
  Nicholas, s. of Martin   56
Attarpyle see Pyle
Aunger, Margaret, abbess of
    Canonsleigh   51, 68, 74, 80, 84, 94,
      101, 106, 109, 119
Aunsel
  Agnes   109
  Robert   120
Aysforde
  Arthur de   54
  John de   21, 54
  John, s. of William   54
  William de   54

Bakere, John   110
Baldewine, Adam   51, 65

Barlahille, John   76
Barre, John atte   71
Bastard, Richard   55
Bath & Wells, bp of see Burnell, Robert
Bathe, Roger   71
Batyn
  Mabel   103, 113, 114
  Walter   89
  William   101
    heirs of   106
Bearde, William   63
Beauchamp, Mary, abbess of
    Canonsleigh   73
Berdeslegh
  Roger de   55
  Thomas   57
Bereholte, Joan Flourette de   112
Bernard, William   102
Bernevile, Henry de   29, 80, 83
Betoun, Stephen   115
Bloyou, Simon   55
Bogeweye, Geoffrey   77
Boltere, Walter   111
Borgh, John   104, 113
Bosco
  Amice, w. of William de senior   56
  William de, heirs of   56, 57
  Stephen de   32, 93
  William de   57
  William de, senior   56
  William, s. of William de, heirs of   56
Boylonde see Bylonde
Braz, Gregory   76
Breye, Simon   65
Brickelbanke, Nicholas   42
Broke, William atte   78

INDEX OF PLACES

Where a modern place name can readily be identified then it is used. If the medieval spelling varies then the alternative spellings follow within parentheses. Wherever possible the place names provided by Vera London in the *Cartulary* are used. No attempt has been made to list all the individual names for fields or small plots of land. Thus any entry in the extents saying 'in <name of field/plot>' will not be itemised. Those entries that say 'at' a certain place are itemised unless they clearly refer to a field, e.g. 'at Holemede', 'at la Deremede'. Such distinctions cannot, however, be clear-cut. The county names of Devon, Somerset, Essex, Dorset and Suffolk are not listed. Appendix 1 is not captured in the index because the relevant index entries are already provided for the extent of the manor of Netherton.

Abbreviations: archbp–archbishop; b.–brother; bp–bishop; d.–daughter; gd.–grand-daughter; gs.–grandson; n.–note; pr.–prior; s.–son; w.–wife; wid.–widow

DEVON AND CORNWALL
RECORD SOCIETY PUBLICATIONS

Previous volumes are available from Boydell & Brewer Ltd.

A Shelf List of the Society's Collections, ed. S. Stride, revised 1986

New Series

65 *Devon Parish Taxpayers, Vol. 3, Churchstow to Dunkeswell*, ed. Todd Gray, 2022

66 *The Memoir of John Butter: Surgeon, Militiaman, Sportsman and Founder of the Plymouth Royal Eye Infirmary*, ed. Dee and Mike Tracey, 2023

67 *Cornish Churches in the Nineteenth Century: The Church Notes of the Lysons Brothers and Sir Stephen Glynne, Volume 1: A-L*, ed. Paul Cockerham, 2024

Devon Maps and Map-Makers: Manuscript Maps before 1840; Supplement to Volumes 43 and 45, ed. Mary R. Ravenhill and Margery M. Rowe, 2010

Extra Series

1 *Exeter Freemen 1266–1967*, ed. Margery M. Rowe and Andrew M. Jackson, 1973

2 *Guide to the Parish and Non-parochial Registers of Devon and Cornwall 1538–1837*, ed. Hugh Peskett, 1979, supplement 1983

3 *William Birchynshaw's Map of Exeter, 1743*, ed. Richard Oliver, Roger Kain and Todd Gray, 2019